"Something inside us longs to be God-ing is the existence we 'post-everythir [...] pursuit is exhausting. What if we admit that God alone is God-like? What if we accept the good limitations of how he created us? That's what *Faithfully Present* helps us to see, as Adam Ramsey guides us into those green pastures and beside those still waters."

Ray Ortlund, President, Renewal Ministries

"In *Faithfully Present*, Adam Ramsey ranges far and wide across time and space: from the apparently insignificant minutiae of our lives to the sweeping realities of the new heavens and the new earth. The pulsing challenge at the heart of the book is to find our contentment and satisfaction not in ourselves (whether our activity or achievements or even relationships) but in our God: Father, Son and Spirit. This is a book to make us stop and think, which, for all of us, is an increasingly pressing need."

Gary Millar, Principal, Queensland Theological College, Australia; Author, *Read This First: A Simple Guide to Getting the Most from the Bible*

"In a world that constantly tells us we can be anything we want to be and to go harder, to run faster and to do more, Adam Ramsey warmly points us back to what's true: we are creatures limited by both time and place. And our limitations are for our good. Adam's words graciously correct our drive to identify with our productivity and to be everywhere all at once. But he doesn't stop there. He invites us to consider how our given limitations set us free to be faithfully present right when and where our good God has placed us. I closed this book with a renewed affection for my family and friends, my faith and my work, the season I'm in, the place I live, the body I've been given, and the heaven that awaits me. This book is full of worshipful words for a weary generation."

Jen Oshman, Author, *Enough about Me; Cultural Counterfeits;* and *Welcome*

"In *Faithfully Present*, Adam Ramsey proves to be a reliable, insightful, and frequently playful guide who helps us navigate the changing seasons of our lives. This book is a heartfelt magnification of the unchanging God, who is faithful and with us through them all."

Jared C. Wilson, Assistant Professor of Pastoral Ministry and Author-in-Residence, Midwestern Seminary; Author, *Love Me Anyway*

"*Faithfully Present* is a refreshing tonic for the soul wearied by our culture's call to do more, be more and achieve more. Beautifully written and packed with theological riches, it is an invitation to receive the limits of time and place as gracious gifts from an infinitely wise and loving Father. Adam shows how embracing these limits is the pathway to greater peace and deeper joy. His call to slow down and live fully present is desperately needed and delightfully liberating."

Carolyn Lacey, Author, *Extraordinary Hospitality (for Ordinary People)* and *Say the Right Thing*

"Adam has given us a lovely meditation on time, bracing reflections on death, and important insights on place. With many turns of phrase, astute observations, and theological gems, *Faithfully Present* beckons us into true living. I am grateful to have read it, and I hope to live better because of it."

Jonathan K. Dodson, Author, *Our Good Crisis* and *The Unwavering Pastor*

"You cannot make time to read this wonderfully pastoral and theologically rich book. But that's the point. We cannot make time; only God can. In our hurried, harried and distracted world, Adam Ramsey offers us a glimpse into a life lived faithfully and present-ly before God. With typical pastoral insight, Adam presents us with a picture of what an embodied, time-honouring, eternity-focused, faithfully present life looks like. And it looks like Jesus! As Adam shows, rather than us becoming frustrated, angry or despairing by our lack of time or the presence of our limits, we have a God who calls us to bring those lacks and limits to him, and who enables us to live faithfully present lives as we wait for time to end and eternity to begin. Take the time to read it!"

Stephen McAlpine, Director for Cultural Engagement, City to City Australia; Author, *Being the Bad Guys*

"So many people are captivated by answering one important identity question: 'Who am I?' While that is an important question, it can't be fully answered without also knowing when you are and where you are. In *Faithfully Present*, Adam Ramsey reminds us of our humanity and our limits. Embracing our humanity helps us embrace our limitless God. I hope this book gets a wide reading."

J.T. English, Lead Pastor, Story Line Church, Arvada, Colorado; Author, *Deep Discipleship*

"Adam Ramsey is quickly becoming one of my favorite authors. After writing deeply and beautifully about the collision of head and heart in *Truth on Fire*, he turns his biblically saturated imagination to a topic we are in desperate need of understanding in our technological age: the truth of limits and how embracing them settles our soul into the present, where we can commune deeply with God and others. In fact the only place where we can do that is in the present. If you feel hurried and thin, or if you feel like your mind is never with you in the room... this is the book for you!"

Matt Chandler, Lead Pastor, The Village Church, Flower Mound, Texas

"Adam has blessed us with such a gift in this book. *Faithfully Present* is beautifully written and deeply convicting, yet packed with hope and joy. Don't rush it. Don't skim it. Take your time and sit with it. Engage with these pages at the heart level...and watch what God does in your life through it."

Dai Hankey, Founder, Red Community; Author, *Hopeward: Gospel Grace for Weary Souls*

To my dad, Brad Ramsey—
for embodying in the lives of your own sons
what you never quite received as a son yourself:
the faithful presence of a good father.
I love you and honour you.
Thank you.

Faithfully Present

Adam Ramsey

thegoodbook
COMPANY

Faithfully Present
© Adam Ramsey, 2023

Published by:
The Good Book Company

thegoodbook.com | thegoodbook.co.uk
thegoodbook.com.au | thegoodbook.co.nz | thegoodbook.co.in

ISBN: 9781784988920 | JOB-007203 | Printed in Turkey

Design by André Parker

Contents

Foreword

by Alex Early

Are you here? I don't mean are you breathing, holding a book in your hand and reading words. I mean does your life whisper, "I'm absent" or shout from deep within your belly, "I am here! Really here! Fully alive to this moment"? In the final moments of your life, will you be saddened because you missed the point or filled with gratitude because you chose to forgo the petty for the sake of the true, good, meaningful, beautiful and, ultimately, eternal? A distracted life is a kind of death before death. A present life is life before Life.

What you're holding is an unusual book of wisdom. And as you've likely learned throughout the course of your life, wisdom is anything but trite, common or easy to come by. Rather, it is almost always forged through shivering winters of pain and scorching summers of heartache.

In 2015, I was working as hard as I could, doing absolutely everything that I believed God had called and equipped me to do. I was surrounded by men and women who affirmed me and cheered me on. I felt like my vision was clear, and I was basking in the sheer favor of the Lord. My first book, *The Reckless Love of God*, was set to release and I was preaching at conferences, developing leaders, and nearing the completion of my doctoral studies. All of my heroes had become my friends. By all accounts, I was thriving—until one Friday afternoon in April, when the sky went black and everything came crashing down.

I walked into my house to learn that my wife of eleven years, who had loved, supported and cherished me, was all but done with faith and church, and even with us. I was more than surprised. I was shocked, crushed, devastated. How? How had I reached the point where the person to whom I'd pledged my very life was suddenly saying these things—and I hadn't seen it coming? Here's how: I deceived myself though "successful" ministry. I mistook large crowds for fruitfulness. I mistook caffeine for the Holy Spirit. I was more interested in being used by God than known by him. I had the veneer of presence but was actually absent. I was in a daydream. Ambition that is fueled, tamed and tempered by the Holy Spirit will lead to a life that honors God, yourself and others. Ambition that is rooted in childhood wounds, the need to be liked and crooked pride is a death grip.

My wife, Jana, and I went on a ministry hiatus for over a year. We submitted ourselves to godly counsel, professional therapy and countless hours of solitude and prayer. We had no idea what shape our lives would take. We discovered that the words the prophet Isaiah spoke about Jesus himself would become true in our own experience of him so many centuries later: "A bruised reed he will not break, and a smoldering wick he will not snuff out" (Isaiah 42:3, NIV). We learned countless lessons through that season of life, giving us what we call around our house the "Early Code". It's our simple mantra, which roots us in a life of faithful presence.

First, all of our wealth is in our relationships. Our relationships with Jesus, each other, our kids and our friends are what is of highest value in our lives. Not our income, square footage, education or whatever else we might be tempted to believe brings true wealth.

Second, Jesus is gentle. Have you met someone who knows how to slow down and spend time with Jesus? Have you ever thought to ask that person, "Well, what's he like?" Here's what I've found: people who know Jesus personally tend to describe him in terms of his gentleness, kindness, compassion and patience. I almost never hear words like "Well, he's Lord, King and Christ". Those things are the obvious titles that Jesus deserves. After all, he did rise from the dead. Yet, at the same time, those who walk closely with him know him as gentle. He said as much about himself (Matthew 11:29).

Third, we aim to live and die in a state of gratitude. Entitlement kills everything, especially relationships and creativity. Remaining in a place of gratitude causes joy to increase as we are set free by the simple words, "Thank you". A life of faithful presence is a thank-you note to God and the world around you.

You will find each of these principles woven throughout *Faithfully Present*. Adam has joined the off-key band of those of us who live our lives upside down, exchanging ambition for faithfulness, being present to where and when we are, rooted in what Jesus describes as abundance (John 10:10). Having known Adam for many years, I can honestly say that this man and his family strive to embody what's written on these pages.

Under the Kindness,
ALEX EARLY
Pastor, Redemption Church Seattle

Learning to Live Where You Are

"We live the given life, not the planned."
WENDELL BERRY

Where and when are you? Come with me on a quick mental field trip through your present time and place.

Where in the world are you sitting right now to read these words? Try to picture your exact location on the globe. Then zoom in: name the town or city you are in. Consider the geographic makeup of how the land rises and falls and how the various bodies of water punctuate and define the surrounding land. Now consider the people who live in that place with you and the countless individual stories that have all woven together to create a shared sense of history and culture in that place.

The more you think about it, the more astounding that place becomes. Yet that place—with its name and geography and quirks and story—is merely one place among 4.3 million unique towns and places on this planet.[1] And we haven't even begun to consider how this blue orb of water and rock, bearing the miraculously precise conditions necessary to sustain life, is at this very moment hurtling at the speed of 110,000 km per hour through space around the sun, while spinning like a basketball on a giant invisible finger at the leisurely pace of approximately 1,600 km per hour.

And somehow, there you sit. Reading a book. Not freaking out about that. Have you really given thought to *where you are?*

Next question: when are you?

Look outside and note the colour of the trees and the patterns of the weather and what that tells you about the season you are in. Name the present year, as recorded by the number of solar laps we've done since the incarnation of Jesus Christ split time in two. Think about the times that have led up to this exact moment in your life. What decade were you born in? What were the fashion trends, music and global events that we now identify with *that* decade? Now try, if you can, to visualise the events from January 1st, 1900 to December 31st, 1999...

The complexity is staggering.

And yet, that century, so filled with world-shaping events and technological advancements, ticked by one minute at a time. Just like our present one is. Zoom in back to this present moment. Look at the watch on your wrist or the clock on your nearest device and take note of the time.

Wherever you are, that place is to you, *here.*

Whenever you are, that time is to you, *now.*

MAKING PEACE WITH OUR HUMANITY

The reality of our time and place is at once blindingly obvious and yet at the same time hardly noticed by us. And yet, isn't it true that the *here* and *now* of where God has us is so frequently the very thing that frustrates us? *Here* and *now* locates us. And that's fine—so long as our present moment is beautiful and fun and untarnished by trouble. But the moment that the vibrant beauty of our highlights in time and place becomes ordinary again, when our present moment is intruded upon by difficulty, when we find our days blurring into one another as we busily rush from one thing to the next—just trying to keep up, living but hardly feeling *alive*—our locatedness feels like a burden to be unloaded. We attempt to escape from and transcend our *here* and *now*, longing for some other *there* and *then*. Our limits become a binding to be stretched, as we seek to fit in *just a little bit more*. And the 21st century provides us with all sorts of technological innovations that promise to enable us to do just that.

Yet here's what I think a lot of us have begun to suspect, deep down, perhaps in sacred moments of clarity, after we surface from the social media fog of our phones: *the need to transcend time and place ruins us for our own time and place.* If we constantly have our minds set on the next thing or another place, we miss the life God has actually given us, even as we keep existing our way through it. On the flip side, it is when we embrace our God-given limitations, being faithfully present to what God desires to do in us and through us, that we become most truly alive. It is when we recognise our humanity—our finite creatureliness—that we feel most truly ourselves.

After all, when good parents place limitations on their children, it's because they love them. And God is a very good Father. His limitations lead to life. As author Zack Eswine reminds us, it was the rejection of God's limitations that broke the world back in Genesis 3, when the hands of the first people stretched out to grasp what should have rightly remained beyond their reach: "'Unlimit me ... for God's glory in my generation!' we might say. But when 'unlimit me' becomes our prayer, we are not the first to pray it. A desire like 'unlimit me, now!' ruined Eden in the first place and bid Jesus to come and die for us."[2] Is it any wonder that every attempt by humanity to play God actually dehumanises us?

So many of our problems, fears, frustrations and anxieties are the result of trying to rid ourselves of what Jesus gladly took upon himself: *humanity.* Far from being a problem to be solved or an obstacle to be overcome, humanity is the very thing that the Lord Jesus entered into when he came into this world:

The Word became flesh and dwelt among us, and we have
seen his glory, glory as of the only Son from the Father, full
of grace and truth. (John 1:14)

While it's true (as we'll see) that you really are much smaller
and more limited than it is comfortable to admit out loud,
you are, yet, most wondrously *here*. God has placed you where
you are, and when you are, for his glory, right now. What if
you made peace with that?

Both your joy and your longevity lie in embracing a life that
loudly declares, "I am not God". That confession—and the
freedom it brings—is the goal of this book.

My hope through these pages is to help you think deeply
and biblically and honestly about the genuine limitations of
time and place that mark your creatureliness. To poke you
with the right words so that you will step back and give weight
to the limited number of sunsets and sabbath days you will
receive and the limited number of places you can inhabit, and
for you to make peace with your "not-Godness" in both of
those realities.

I want you to have your eyes open to *here* and *now* in the
ever-changing seasons and spaces of your life. To glorify God
right where you are, not where you think you ought to be. To
be present to the life that you *do* have, not the life you think
you *should* have. As the poet-farmer Wendell Berry reminded
us right at the beginning of this chapter, "We live the given
life, and not the planned".[3] When we learn to master our
ambitions, rather than being mastered by them, we find
ourselves discovering, alongside the apostle Paul, the secret
superpower of *contentment*.

I have learned to be content in whatever circumstances
I find myself. I know how to make do with little, and
I know how to make do with a lot. In any and all
*circumstances I have learned **the secret of being content***

... I am able to do all things through him who strengthens me. (Philippians 4:11-13, CSB, emphasis added)

What powered Paul onwards was knowing that the risen Jesus was ever near and ever strong. Because he was convinced that "the Lord is near" (v 5, CSB), he was "invincibilised" with contentment. That's what we're aiming for.

MOVING FORWARD BY STAYING PRESENT

In the chapters that follow, we are going to explore how the Scriptures speak to two powerful realities that limit us and locate us: time and space—the "whens" and the "wheres" of our current existence. What I am arguing for can really be summarised in the two-word phrase coined by the American scholar James Davison Hunter: *faithful presence.* Here's how Hunter defines this concept:

> At root, a theology of faithful presence begins with an acknowledgement of God's faithful presence to us and that his call upon us is that we be faithfully present to him in return. This is the foundation, the logic, the paradigm ... Only by being fully present to God as a worshipping community and as adoring followers can we be faithfully present in the world."[4]

In other words, the more our lives are oriented by the faithful presence of God to us, we too will become attentive and present to one another.

Isn't that—life with God that we are fully alive to—what we most want to know? A life in which success is measured less by numerical data and more by relational flourishing— vertically with God and horizontally with others. Where churches seek to be, as my friend Alex Early describes it, "a community of people who are faithfully present to God, self, and others".[5]

The first part of this book will outline various aspects of time, along with biblical reflections on what faithfulness to God looks like in those times. How do we live faithfully when life keeps changing? When life moves slowly? When life is coming at us fast? When life comes to an end?

The second part of the book focuses on the different spaces and places that *locate* us. God has given you one body, which can live in one place at a time, with a web of relationships to other people around you in that place. And in Christ, you are on your way home—heaven-bound—even as the kingdom of heaven gradually yet inevitably breaks into this world.

And that is where we will end: staring at the staggering reality of what is coming our way in the new creation, when earth and heaven become one place. There is indeed coming a moment in our definite future when time as we know it will be unlimited and place as we experience it will be uncursed. The limits will be lifted as we enter into fullness of life, unpunctuated by death, forever with God.

But here and now, we are to live each of our present days in light of the "eternal weight of glory beyond all comparison" (2 Corinthians 4:17) that is in our future. And as we do, we learn to remember that each of the spaces we inhabit, and the times in which we do so, come to us from the hand of God. What would this coming week look like—all the gloriously ordinary parts of it you have planned for, along with some of the predictably unpredictable parts that no one can plan for—if you were to receive it, moment by moment, attentive to God's presence and God's purposes throughout it? The 2nd-century church father Irenaeus famously wrote, "The glory of God is man fully alive".[6] That's what every one of us wants down at the core of who we are: to be faithfully present and fully alive to God, right here and right now, with every part of our lives.

Part 1:
Time

CHAPTER ONE

TIME
A Precious Enigma

"In the beginning, God created the heavens and the earth."
GENESIS 1:1

Where do we begin with time? Well, in the beginning. When we consider the opening of the creation account in Genesis 1:1, most of us naturally think in terms of "matter". We imagine God making the physical components of reality: all the tangible things and touchable stuff that make up creation. What we often overlook, however, is that when God created the world, the universe and existence as we know it, he also created time.

Let's take a quick road trip back to one of your high-school science classes, where "Mr K" or "Ms B" hurt your brain by introducing you to the complexity of physics. Scientists tell us that the fundamental elements of the universe are time, space, matter and energy. These four components interact with one another to give us reality as we know it. And while physicists and super-geniuses (and guys in the YouTube comment sections) wrestle with how to integrate Einstein's theory of general relativity with quantum mechanics to give us a coherent, all-encompassing "theory of everything", the opening words of the Bible reveal something that is as profoundly simple as it is simply profound.

In the beginning, God created the heavens and the earth.
(Genesis 1:1)

God is the supreme source of energy, who is powering existence (or, to borrow the words of the Greek philosopher Aristotle, he is the "prime Mover" or the "uncaused Cause"). He is the eternal, self-existing and single ultimate reality, whose existence is the basis of all other existence—that is, of time, space, and matter. Each of these factors make up the substance of our lives, while also giving limits to our lives.

Matter and space are relatively straightforward to get our heads around: matter is the concrete physical stuff we see around us, while space has to do with the location of matter in relation to other matter.

But what exactly is time? And why does it haunt us so powerfully?

THE ENIGMA OF TIME

That first question is harder to answer than you might think. Put simply, the concept of time has to do with the *sequence* and *duration* with which matter interacts with other matter. But our experience of that sequence remains annoyingly enigmatic. Are we being carried along in time, moving forward into the future with each tick of the clock? Or is time flowing backward, from a fluid future into a concretised-past?

Consider these two equally viable definitions of time in respected dictionaries:

1. Merriam-Webster: Time is a "continuum that is measured in terms of events which succeed one another from past through present to future".

2. The World English Dictionary: Time is "the continuous passage of existence in which events pass from a state of

potentiality in the future, through the present, to a state of finality in the past".

If that seeming contradiction frustrates you, you're in good company. Time has puzzled our deepest thinkers and philosophers since, well, the beginning of time. The 20th-century Russian novelist Vasily Grossman captured the mystery and tension of time well when he wrote:

> Time is a transparent medium. People and cities arise out of it, move through it and disappear back into it. It is time that brings them and time that takes them away … Such is time: everything passes, it alone remains; everything remains, it alone passes. And how swiftly and noiselessly it passes.[7]

HOW TIME HAUNTS US

Perhaps the unbending enigmacity of time is what causes our haunted experience of it and fuels our obsession with obtaining more of it. Thousands of self-help books are printed each year teaching you how to manage your time. Health gurus recommend diets and training rhythms so that you can attempt to extend your time. Storytellers provoke us to imagine ways in which we can control time. From the time machine of novelist H.G. Wells to Marty McFly's time-travelling DeLorean sports car in *Back to the Future*, to the Time-Turner used by Harry Potter, or the Time Stone guarded by Doctor Strange in the Marvel movies, we dream of ways in which we can transcend the limit of time.

And there's a reason for all of that.

Time is precious.

To us, time is the currency of life, which is why we spend it. Whether it flows forward or backward is utterly irrelevant at the level of our lived experience. All we know is that it is indeed flowing past us, with irreversible permanence. After all, it was only yesterday that you were a child, carefree and filled with innocent wonder at the workings of the world. And now, that time has gone.

Think about some of the important milestones and defining moments of beauty and sorrow that have intersected your timeline thus far. Finishing school. Getting married. Achieving a goal. Becoming a parent. Saying goodbye to a parent. How quickly we arrive at events that once seemed so unbearably distant and far off in our future. How quickly ambitions become memories and the future is remembered in photos.

How does contemplating that make you feel? Anxious? Sad? Determined all the more to make your mark on the present?

How badly we need to lay hold of the trusting perspective of the psalmist:

> *But I trust in you, O LORD;*
> *I say, "You are my God."*
> *My times are in your hand." (Psalm 31:14-15)*

Yet if we want to share the psalmist's trust, we must accept the psalmist's truth. And the truth that those beautiful verses confront us with is the reality that we are not God, and that our time belongs to him.

Let me say it more bluntly: you are not that big a deal, and you're going to die soon.

YOU ARE NOT THAT BIG A DEAL, AND YOU'RE GOING TO DIE SOON

You are not that big a deal. Hear me out. I'm not saying you don't matter. Far from it. It's just that despite the fact that you and I tend to see reality through a lens in which we are the main character of the story, the truth is that we're really not. Author Morgan Housel has pointed out that "Your personal experiences ... make up maybe 0.00000001% of what's happened in the world, but maybe 80% of how you think the world works".[8] In other words, you and I are not central to any of this. We are, as the 1st-century church fathers and modern-day lawyers both like to say, *nihil ad rem*—besides the point.

Stay with me.

I am sure that you are of great significance to those who know and love you. Maybe you even have an online presence with thousands of followers who are eager to hear what you have to say. That's wonderful. Yet, in the grand scheme of things—compared to empire commanders like Alexander and Napoleon, who shaped continents; gospel pioneers like the apostles or George Whitefield or Lottie Moon, who broke new spiritual ground; or thought leaders like Frederick Douglass or Steve Jobs, whose voices and inventions radically moved the needle in their times—you really are very small.

Stay with me. There is some hope coming.

You are going to die soon.

Ok, that last "stay with me" was misleading. And probably a little mean. I really do have some really good news on the way that is brimming with hope; but we need to ensure first that our self-created delusion is sufficiently dead—specifically, the delusion that thinks *death happens to other people*. But death is going to happen to you, me, and everyone else you know. *My time* is one day going to come to an end. And so will yours. As the writer Anne Lamott put it, "In a hundred years? ... All new people."[9]

Which means that everything you've accomplished in the course of your life will likely be entirely forgotten three generations from now. Your life will probably be remembered fondly and deeply by your friends and children. It might be somewhat known by your grandchildren. But you'll be lucky if your great-grandchildren can even recall your full name.

(And if you are upset by that last sentence, see if you can name all eight of *your* great grandparents, including middle names, right now off the top of your head.)

You see? I didn't make the rules. This is just the way things are. You're probably not a world-changer or history-maker or planet-shaker or whatever else the guy on stage told you at youth camp. And neither am I.

But I'm ok with that.

Just because you and I are not that big a deal in the grand sweep of God's redemptive plan, that does not mean we don't matter. You are made in the image of God, you are loved by Jesus, and you have been custom designed for a specific set of purposes on this planet, at this very moment in history, that are ordained of God. You deeply matter. You're just not the central character. For while God's story includes you, it's not about you. *It's about him.* And it's in making peace with that reality that we find ourselves able to say with the psalmist, "I trust in you, O LORD ... My times are in your hand" (Psalm 31:14-15).

THE KING OF ALL TIME

The reason why we can trust God with our time is that he alone stands outside of it. Part of *our* difficulty with understanding time is that we are always looking at it from within—like goldfish in a bowl trying to make sense of water. What we need is an external perspective on time from the only perfectly objective Being who stands outside of it. And that, Scripture tells us, is who God is:

> *¹ Lord, you have been our refuge in every generation.*
> *² Before the mountains were born,*
> *before you gave birth to the earth and the world,*
> *from eternity to eternity, you are God.*
> *³ You return mankind to the dust, saying,*
> *"Return, descendants of Adam."*

⁴ For in your sight a thousand years are like yesterday
that passes by,
like a few hours of the night" (Psalm 90:1-4, CSB).

God is ever present to every generation (v 1). God is the eternal one, the cause of creation itself (v 2)—the first and the last, as Isaiah puts it (Isaiah 44:6; 48:12). God preceded the birth of time, and God will outlast the end of time. In Psalm 90:2-3, Moses compares God's eternality with our mortality, reminding us of the brevity with which each of us exists in time. Then, in verse 4, he again speaks of God's ever-present timelessness. Each millennium recorded in human history, each multigenerational dynasty ruled by kings and queens and caesars and emperors, is to God "like a few hours of the night". In the divine scheme of things, the two and a half centuries that mark the entire history of the United States are to God little more than an episode on Netflix that you watched last weekend. What is a thousand years—what is all of human history—but different ends of the same page of paper, held by the hand of he who holds all things.

We are much smaller and more fleeting than we realise: beings within time who belong to time. But time belongs to God. He is the is the "King of Ages" (1 Timothy 1:17), which means he not only reigns over time as a whole but also over *your time*: that is, over the beginning and end dates of every created thing, including you.

Life is a symphony of events occurring and colliding with one another in time and space, and God is the conductor. The song of creation moves at his tempo, rising and falling with the pace of his rhythm. And when all is completed, the people of God will look back on God's story—upon the song we call "time"—and marvel. Even the minor chords of our sufferings, when heard from within the full symphony of God's purposes, will become to us unexpected harmonies.

Here and now, God wants us to trust him with the final musical arrangement and be faithful with our part—to learn to live in our time, at his pace, according to his design, because we know that the King of the ages will indeed make "everything beautiful in its time" (Ecclesiastes 3:11). When we believe that that is true, we can accept the limits woven into our humanity—that we are finite, needy and located beings—not as obstacles to overcome, but as part of God's grace. Our relative obscurity and finitude in the grand scheme of things need not depress us. On the contrary, it is through embracing our limits that we discover true freedom.

THE GRACE OF LIMITEDNESS

"You don't have to be the best at everything."

"Learn to laugh at yourself."

"Know your limits."

Each of these phrases has been cemented in my memory, repeated countless times to me by my father during my childhood and teenage years. As the ultra-competitive, win-at-all-costs, eldest of four brothers, not one of these important lessons was learned quickly. That's probably because they all had to do with humility—a virtue that came to me about as naturally as Latin does to a duck.

While it is true that none of us can really say, "I am humble!" without ironically wrecking the said humility, it is nonetheless something that we are called to pursue (Philippians 2:3-8). And at the heart of seeking humility is embracing the limits of our humanity. Our natural tendency is to attempt to be what God alone can be: *omnipresent* or *all-present*. God is limitlessly and effortlessly present not only in every created place but in every created moment. His fullness dwells not only in every *where* but in every *when*.

At the risk of stating the obvious, we are not all-present. In fact, we can't even be fully present in *two* places at the same time, let alone in many places or all places. Place, along with time, locates us (something we will explore more fully later in the book). And despite our attempts to be in multiple spaces at once through social media, technology or the illusion of multitasking, we are bounded creatures, confined to the limits of one body, inhabiting one place at any one moment in time. When we try to be otherwise, we only sabotage our joy and growth in our present time and place. As the 1st-century Roman philosopher Seneca reminds us, "To be everywhere is to be nowhere".[10]

In light of this, why is it so difficult for us to be present? Instead of savouring the present, which touches our senses for only a moment of time, why do our minds so compulsively wander to the next meeting on the calendar, or the bill we need to pay, or the mess we need to fix, or the event we need to attend? The real trouble with all our attempts to be technologically omnipresent in multiple spaces is that we fail to be fully present in any space. We become digitally distracted—physically near those we love yet so often mentally absent.

Allow me another slightly confronting thought experiment to bring home how back to front this really is. Imagine the final moments of your life. Consider who you would want to have in the room, physically near you. Why have we allowed it to become normal to so frequently give *those* people our physical presence but mental absence, as we strive to be digitally present to people on our social-media feeds who likely won't even enter our mind in our final hours, let alone our hospital room?

There must be another way. What if our ability to be present only in one moment at a time was part of God's grace to us? What if rejoicing in our limitedness was the pathway to a peaceful heart and unworried mind?

We are unipresent; God alone is omnipresent. We are finite—our time is limited; God alone is infinite. He alone inhabits every time and place, and he does so perfectly. Were we to inhabit a godless universe, we would have every reason to despair over the irretrievable passing of time. But time is not flowing backward into a pointless past, nor is it flowing forward into an uncertain future. Time belongs to the God who made its beginning and is sovereign over its end—and who will bring us, one day, to our eternal home with him: a perpetual springtime and unending day, where time, as we presently understand it, will no longer be governed by the inevitability of endings but shall gallop onward for ever into a deathless future of no regrets. Time need not haunt you, when you know it does not hold you. For the one who holds time holds your life. You can trust him with your time because he is reigning over all of time.

In the beginning, God created the heavens and the earth.
(Genesis 1:1)

CHAPTER TWO

TIMES
Chronos and Kairos

*"All we have to decide is what to do with the time
that is given us."*
J.R.R. TOLKIEN

Picture two men. One is old and fearsome: a merciless ruler who takes every thing from every creature—whoever lives within his realm. His determination is unbending: his consistency as unyielding as the grave. More than that, he is the doorman of the grave. In one hand he holds a scythe: in the other an hourglass. *The* hourglass. And he makes no exceptions.

The second man is young and playful—mischievous even. While the old man plods, the young man dances. Never will you find him standing still. He, too, takes orders from no one but dares you to grab hold of him by the hair, if you can. Like an 80s punk rocker, his hair is long at the front and shaved at the back because whoever desires to take hold of him must do so head on. For once his nimble feet have passed you by, he can never be caught from behind.

To the ancient Greeks, the old man was the god Chronos, from whom our more modern depictions of Father Time and the Grim Reaper are drawn. The young guy with the quick feet and reverse mullet was Kairos. They were the personifications of two Greek words—*chronos* and *kairos*—that help us understand that there is *time* (*chronos*) and *times* (*kairos*). Much of what follows in the chapters ahead will explore the latter. But we need to understand both because God reigns over both. And it's only as we grasp this that we can begin to relate to chronos and kairos not with fear or frustration but with freedom and joy.

CHRONOS: A HISTORY OF TIME

Chronos can be defined as "clock time"—the seconds, minutes, hours, days, weeks, months and years of life. It's where we get our word "chronological" from: the order and sequence of events that we refer to as "time". When the Scriptures speak of Jesus seeing a man who had been paralysed for 38 years lying at the pool of Bethsaida, and says that he had "been there a long time" (John 5:5-6), or when Jesus says to his disciples, "I will be with you a little longer," (7:33), "chronos" is the Greek word being used. Chronos is about duration and sequence. And for those of us living in more Westernised contexts, we're obsessed with trying to measure it and order our lives by those measurements. Our fixation with time can be traced back to the invention and evolution of the clock.

For thousands of years, our ancestors employed sundials and waterclocks and hourglasses to measure the larger portions of a "day", but time was primarily regulated by the rising and setting of the sun. Then came the 6th-century monastic communities of Benedict of Nursia. Desiring not to waste God's time, these monks implemented a rule of life that divided the day with seven calls to prayer. Before long, bells were used to mark the beginning of each new activity or spiritual discipline. As historian Lewis Mumford insightfully points out, "The clock is not merely a means of keeping track of the hours, but of synchronizing the actions of men".[11]

By the late 14th-century, this was no longer true just of the monasteries. Mechanised church bells ringing out from the centre of European towns, on the hour every hour, regulated and harmonised a community's shared sense of time. Large and beautiful clocks could be seen in the centre of every self-respecting city and town across the continent. And as the bells chimed hour after hour, day after day, another subtle shift was taking place: "Eternity ceased to serve as the measure and focus of human events".[12]

Soon these clocks were shrunk down to fit into living rooms, and before long, they began to inhabit coat pockets and travel on human wrists. And the rest, as they say, is history.

Today, our lives are ordered by the clock. The advancement of time-keeping technology has revolutionised the world, improving and effectively organising many areas of society. But it came at a cost. The more we counted the seconds, the more we tried to squeeze into them. The more we put ourselves under the eye of time, the more power we gave to it. We forgot that Chronos is a taker and insatiably greedy.

Notice the progression: first, clocks were centralised. Then they were personalised. Next, they were miniaturised. And before we knew it, Chronos had been idolised. Or, as the author Neil Postman quipped, "The clock made us into time-keepers, and then time-savers, and now time-servers".[13] Those hands that marked the minutes and hours, ever-racing around the face of the clock, reached out and took hold of us, sweeping us into their orbit, breathless and hurried.

Now we even say that "time is money". Chronos has been commodified and is ultimate in value—which is why we think of time as something that we *spend* rather than a gift we have received. For just like money, when Time is made ultimate, he is a ruthless master.

Chronos is the non-negotiating, unrelenting *tick, tick, tick, tick, tick, tick, tick, tick, tick, tick, tick, tick, tick,*

tick, tick, tick, tick, tick, tick, tick, tick, tick, tick, tick, tick, tick, tick, tick, tick of the clock, in which your earthly life appears, ticks away for a little while and then is no more… The clock continues to *tick* ever onward, never slowing, forever colonising each of your lived moments into the unassailable kingdom of "the Past".

Now, in the unlikely event that one or two or every single one of you skimmed that last sentence after the third or fourth *tick* and didn't actually read the complete sequence of words (no judgment here—I would have done the same!), then please reread it, one word at a time. You missed something. Here it is again; read it slowly, at clock-ticking speed.

Chronos is the non-negotiating, unrelenting *tick, tick* of the clock, in which your earthly life appears, ticks away for a little while, and then is no more… The clock continues to *tick* ever onward, never slowing, forever colonising each of your lived moments into the unassailable kingdom of "the Past".

Have you realised what you missed while you read that sentence? Here's what: roughly about a minute of your life. One unrecoverable minute gone. And I tricked you into doing it twice (sorry about that).

Quantifying our time is an attempt to give us a measure of control over it. Yet though we have divided it and measured it, chronos refuses to be mastered. Time-management techniques? I don't think so. You may manage your *response* to events in your life; you may direct your limited energy and attention as best you can; but we may as well talk about techniques for managing the intensity of the sun or the fury of an F5 tornado before we talk about ordering Chronos around. For though we continue to try, no mortal manages time.

KAIROS: THE RIGHT TIME

But not all time is like that. Kairos time is something different entirely. Kairos is not really about duration but *timeliness*. Moments in time that are just the right moment at just the right time. Seasons of time that are an "appointed season". Opportunities realised and life lived as it ought to be. The Latin phrase *carpe diem*—seize the day—speaks to the defining moments of kairos time that must be grabbed hold of as they approach us. The main idea here is *ripeness*.

Like a time of unhurried storytelling and laughter among friends.

Like stepping into a vocation that you were born to do.

Like the healing tears that come with forgiveness.

Like the wonder of becoming a parent.

Like a perfect mango.

Have you ever tasted a mango at the appointed stage of its perfection, ripely soft in glorious reds and yellows? It's one of the most exquisite flavours on earth. Have you ever tasted an unripe mango, hard and green and bitter? It's like biting into an angry lime, drunk on vinegar, committed to destroying all joy in your life. The difference is kairos—the right time.

Not all chronos time is kairos time. But every kairos time occurs within chronos time. And when it does, we often forget about time entirely. So engaged are we in *the right thing at the right time* that hours fly past us like fleeting moments. And not only are we not bothered by that; we delight in such times and gladly exclaim things like "Where has the time gone?!" or "Time flies when you're having fun!"

Those of us in Western cultures tend to live more chronologically dominated lives than relationally oriented ones. But that's not true everywhere. In some places—like parts of Africa and many of the islands in the Pacific and the Caribbean—life is ordered far more relationally. Perhaps you've experienced "African time" or "island time", as it is commonly called? It has more of a kairos flavour to it. To ask, "When will this finish?" or "What time will we begin?" is like asking, "How wet is the water?" It will finish when it is over. It will begin when it's the right time to begin. It's not that such cultures don't have watches or calendars or schedules. They do. It's just that people are less subservient to the devices of chronos.

Chronos asks, "How much time?"

Kairos asks, "Is it time?"

Chronos plods, never stopping.

Kairos dances, never staying.

Chronos is what we are afraid to lose.

Kairos is what we are afraid to miss.

And both chronos and kairos belong to Jesus, serving his purposes, just as he intends them to.

SERVING JESUS, THE LORD OF TIME

Jesus, who preceded time (John 1:2) and who created time (v 3), descended into chronos time in a kairos moment so monumental that today's date is literally based on how many years it's been since he did.

"At just the right time," says Paul in Romans 5:6 (NIV), "... Christ died for the ungodly." Again, he says, "When the fullness of time had come, God sent forth his Son ... so that we might receive adoption as sons" (Galatians 4:4-5). God chose to reveal his love within time by sending Jesus to be born, and to die, and to rise again, at just the right time. His time.

Unlike the Kairos of Greek mythology, who was more mischievous and slippery than Peter Pan's shadow, Jesus doesn't want you to try and catch him. He wants you to trust him. No moral parkour routine to try and keep up with him is necessary; no rolling the dice to guess where he's going to be next is required. Just the hand of faith that reaches out to his, and then walking with him into every day of your chronos life. You need not serve time nor fear its march, when you serve the one whom time serves.

Take a moment to pause and consider what that means for you, here and now. Where does your heart need to remember this anxiety-incinerating truth? You exist within time, but you do not belong to time.

You belong to Jesus.

When you are overwhelmed by the passage of time or underwhelmed with the lack of ripeness that your present season possesses, remind your heart who time itself belongs to. The duration of all time, and of our time, is in God's hands.

That's the key to being free from the tyranny of time, be it chronos or kairos. We just need to see them for what they actually are: not gods to be served but servants of the one true God. Jesus alone is the rightful Lord of time—the "King of ages, immortal, invisible, the only God" (1 Timothy 1:17). Chronos marches on as its Lord intends; kairos dances to the divine rhythm and tempo that he has set. The moments of time that are loaded with meaning are gifts to be received as they come our way. The anxieties we feel from the relentlessness of chronos and the elusiveness of kairos are quelled as we bend our knee to the Lord that they serve. Look at what Peter says:

*Humble yourselves, therefore, under the mighty hand of God so that at **the proper time** he may exalt you, casting all your anxieties on him, because he cares for you.*
(1 Peter 5:6-7, emphasis added)

"At the proper time". The appropriate time; the perfect moment; at just the right time. God will not be one second too early or too late in accomplishing his purposes for every person who humbles themselves before him. And he promises that when we do—when we acknowledge our limitedness and trust him with our time—he will exalt us, at just the right time. Did you catch the magnificence of what Peter just said? The King of time will exalt us. If Peter sounds audacious, we need to remember that he is merely repeating what the Lord Jesus himself promised: "If anyone serves me, the Father will honour him" (John 12:26). When time has run its course and we stand before the Father, there will be no greater privilege in the universe than being honoured by him.

Chronos does not care for you; you are barely a blip on the radar of his long march. Kairos does not care for you; he will leave you again and again, even if you do collide with him occasionally by chance. The posture required to live well within chronos, while dancing open-eyed to kairos, is to bend your knee with them before Jesus. He is the Lord of time, now in your today. He will be in your tomorrow. And you can trust him with all of it "because he cares for you" (1 Peter 5:7).

CHAPTER THREE

SEASONS
Changing Times

*"The sky bright after summer-ending rain,
I sat against an oak half up the climb.
The sun was low; the woods was hushed in shadow;
Now the long shimmer of the crickets' song
Had stopped. I looked up to the westward ridge
And saw the ripe October light again,
Shining through leaves still green yet turning gold.
Those glowing leaves made of the light a place
That time and leaf would leave. The wind came cool,
And then I knew that I was present in
The long age of the passing world, in which
I once was not, now am, and will not be,
And in that time, beneath the changing tree,
I rested in a keeping not my own."*

WENDELL BERRY

Spring. Summer. Autumn. Winter.
  Growth. Maturity. Decline. Death.
Childhood. Adulthood. Middle age. Old age.
Whether it's the patterns of the weather, the phases of an organisation or the stages of life, the wisdom of Ecclesiastes 3:1 rings true: "For everything there is a season, and a time for every matter under heaven." Life is a series of beginnings

and endings. And while change is inevitable, that doesn't mean it is always enjoyable. The uncertainty that comes with new beginnings is a common cause of anxiety. But the very real sense of loss that results from clear and definite endings, when we navigate change that cannot be unchanged, is often nothing short of terrifying. Whether it's moving to a new city, changing jobs, entering a new life-stage or negotiating the shifting dynamics of a friendship, part of learning to live faithfully present in the here and now is knowing how to transition from beginnings to endings to new beginnings.

CONSTANT CHANGE

Have you ever considered that there was a day when Israel— after escaping from Egypt and wandering through the wilderness for 40 years and experiencing God's miraculous daily provision of manna—eventually crossed over into Canaan? On the previous day, they had woken up, gathered up the manna that God had nourished them on for years, and eaten it. Yet on their first morning in the promised land, everything changed. The journey was now over. The manna was now a memory.

> *And the manna ceased the day after they ate of the produce of the land. And there was no longer manna for the people of Israel, but they ate of the fruit of the land of Canaan that year. (Joshua 5:12)*

I wonder what that moment was like? Surely there were many who had taken the miracle of manna for granted. And now it was gone—no longer necessary. And while I'm sure the predominant national mood was one of great joy, do you think it's possible—as the decades rolled by, and they told the stories of God's provision to their children and their children's children—that they missed the gift that had once been so commonplace to them?

Change is one of the constants of time. So embracing the season we are in, rather than the season we wish we were in, is another key to being faithfully present to the life God has given us. The longing to be in some stage of life other than where we presently are is common to all of us. Yet so too is the tendency, when we do eventually find ourselves in a different season, to look back wistfully, wishing we had savoured what we'd once had.

As an example, consider the transitions within the season of parenthood. During her pregnancy, a mother navigates profound changes in her body as the baby develops and the weight of responsibility grows on her through this time— both literally and metaphorically. For new fathers, this time is marked by a wonderful though strange experience of second- hand anticipation of the newness that grows in the womb of our beloved. It is also a time for processing feelings of utter uselessness for alleviating her ever-increasing discomfort, apart from our ability to satisfy the late-night food cravings for fries or slushies, or [insert random food] as a volunteer Uber Eats driver.

And then the child is born, and everything changes. For first-time parents, our joy is matched only by our cluelessness. But we figure it out as we go, like every parent who came before us. During the early years of parenthood when our children are still very young, our day-to-day awareness of time's passage is largely hidden from us, camouflaged in the background of our exhaustion. And then suddenly, apparently without warning, that child is a teenager. And while we don't miss the fatigue of those early years (like, not at all), we do however realise that there were countless things from that time that did not travel with us into our present time. Those moments belonged to a different season. They were limited- edition gifts.

LIMITED-EDITION GIFTS

This came home to me one weekend a few years ago in a profound way. On this evening, our five children (then aged thirteen, eleven and nine, along with a pair of 6-year-old twins) had successfully deployed multiple methods of avoiding going to bed at their allocated time (which fortunately only seems to happen every single day). After finally getting them all into their beds, praying with them and tucking in our younger ones, my wife, Kristina, and I sat on the couch, exhaled a long day, and were able to spend some time together. For about ten minutes. Suddenly, from across the house, we heard the loud voice of a small person, shouting my name.

"Dad. Dad! Daaaaaaad! DAAAAAAAAAAAAAAD!!!!"

I marched into the bedroom, lost my temper, and began the well-rehearsed rant that I'm assuming is familiar to every parent required to deal with a disobedient child after the hour of 9pm.* On this occasion, however, before I could really get my parental rant off the ground, that same little voice interrupted me, looking into my face with wide-eyed sincerity, and said, "Dad, I just really needed another cuddle".

I repented and made restitution with a super-long cuddle (obviously).

Now, did that child of mine play me? Possibly. Ok, fine, very likely. But in that moment, I didn't mind even a little bit because a realisation had caught me emotionally off guard,

---

* *Post-9pm Parent Rant:* For the uninitiated, this well-known bedtime liturgy of the flesh involves a recap of the ways in which you have already served them in the bedtime routine that evening; a second recap of what the family expectations are for bedtimes; a reminder of your love for them, usually spoken in a stern voice; a warning of what will happen if they get out of their bed again; and concludes with, "Good night!". To which the child replies, "Good night." But then the child generally adds another, "I love you." And you repeat, "Love you too" (this time a little bit nicer), because you really do love them. And then you walk away feeling mildly guilty because you know they're just a kid and that you committed the same bedtime felonies in your own childhood, but the guilt recedes quickly because you're tired and you've done a variation of this dance more times than you can remember.

striking me hard and unexpectedly: "There is coming a day when I won't hear that little voice call my name from their bedroom ever again".

The next morning, I posted a reflection on my social media that seemed to resonate widely with parents. Perhaps, like me (and my wife, who read it and punched me), they were caught emotionally off guard by the realisation that seasons come with both beginnings and endings:

To the Weary Parent of a Young Child,

There is coming a day where:

they will climb onto your lap,
they will ask for a shoulder-ride,
they will call your name at night,
they will reach for your hand,

...and it will be the last time.

And neither of you will know it.

We've been granted an unknown yet limited number of these. And what can sometimes feel like an interruption, is actually a limited-edition gift.

This isn't just true of parenthood; every stage of life has its limited-edition gifts. God has woven specific joys into each and every season which are unique to those seasons. And though we try, we cannot hoard these moments. We've all seen the sad futility of someone attempting to live in the past. But real life isn't found in reliving past moments. Instead, we are to accept the limits of each season that passes us by, knowing there are other unique joys woven into the season we are about to enter. I love how author N.D. Wilson helps us delight in these limited-edition gifts:

Having a finite mind when surrounded by joy that is perpetually rolling back into the rear view is like always having something important on the tips of our tongues, something on the tips of our fingers, always slipping away, always ducking our embrace … But this shouldn't inspire melancholy; it should only tinge the sweet with the bitter. Don't resent the moments simply because they cannot be frozen. Taste them. Savor them. Give thanks for that daily bread. Manna doesn't keep overnight. More will come in the morning.[14]

A TIME FOR EVERYTHING

"For everything there is a season, and a time for every matter under heaven" (Ecclesiastes 3:1). So said Solomon, the wisest man to live until Jesus walked the earth. What follows this statement in Ecclesiastes is a poem that simply describes the way that life is. Solomon lays out 14 pairs of opposites which paint the cycles of beginnings and endings that every human being will experience. There is "a time to be born, and a time to die" (v 2); "a time to weep and a time to laugh; a time to mourn, and a time to dance" (v 4); "a time to keep silence, and a time to speak" (v 7)—and so on, with the eventual promise that God makes "everything beautiful in its time" (v 11).

Are you alive to the stage of life you are in? Or are you just ambling through, oblivious to the unrepeatable wonders within it?

Consider for a moment the stages that mark the typical human life. Given that the average lifespan is around 80 years of age (plus or minus a few years, depending on where you live), we can think of it in terms of seasons—four periods of time, roughly 20 years each in length, which give shape to our lives. Each one is beautiful in its time.

The Spring of Childhood (age 0-20). We are taking in God's world one glorious new experience at a time. We are learning who we are and how God has gifted us. Unburdened by the responsibilities of our elders, our imaginations run wild with what the future might be, as we race toward it with boundless energy.

The Summer of Adulthood (age 21-40). The summer of our lives is a season of celebration and defining moments. It is a time when we focus our gifts toward a specific vocational pathway. Many of us will celebrate getting married and raising children. We settle into convictions about what matters most in life. Adulthood marks a time when we are no longer children merely receiving from those around us, but men and women who now meaningfully contribute to the world.

The Autumn of Midlife (age 41-60). Here we enter a season of fullness and maturity. We enjoy the fruit produced from the summer of our life, along with the wisdom and influence we have gained through those years. No longer are we considered by anyone as a young man or woman. Instead, we notice the beginnings of a decline in our energy and strength as this season goes on. The transition is sometimes a difficult one, with many of us navigating health issues or some sort of midlife crisis as it dawns on us that we are now closer to our end than our beginning.

The Winter of Our Final Years (age 61-). The winter of life means that our race is entering the final furlong. We're not dead yet and have plenty left to do, but we are slowing down. The signs are all there: the colour of winter's snow has appeared in our hair, as "a crown of glory" (Proverbs 16:31). We look back on our lives with grateful hearts. Desiring to finish well, we press onward by passing on our gifts and wisdom to those coming up behind us. We prepare for the inevitability of death, even as we look forward with eagerness to the eternal springtime of heaven, now just a little way over the horizon, longing to hear the most precious of words, "Well done, good and faithful servant … Enter into the joy of your master" (Matthew 25:23).

How did you feel as you read about the above seasons? Are you so fixated on seasons behind you or yet ahead of you that your heart is disgruntled by the one staring you in the face? Do you feel envious when you look at the seasons that those around you are in? If God is with you in every season, then there is unimaginable joy and goodness and purpose and meaning and courage to be found in every season. Each stage of our life is unrepeatable. Each is beautiful. The only question is: do we really believe that?

FAITHFULLY PRESENT TO THE SEASON YOU'RE IN

It's as we embrace this that we learn to live well. After all, how many of our frustrations are the result of our attempts to live in a different season to our present one? When we are teenagers, we want to be adults and enjoy the freedoms that come with adulthood. When we are adults, we long for the carefree days of our childhood. I'm sure you can think of countless other examples. Yet while our longings for better days (however we might define that) are understandable, they can be poor companions. They are like that one friend who constantly talks throughout a movie, so busy trying to predict what is coming up or make sense of what happened in the past that they miss the story unfolding in real-time. Always longing to be in a time that is not this time leads to misliving in every time.

So let me ask you again: what season of life are you in— here and now—which God wants you to be fully present to? Fruitfulness over the long haul is a lot less about finding balance and a lot more about knowing what season you are in and living accordingly. Whatever season you're in, do not lose heart. Refuse to quit on your present season just because it doesn't look like a previous one. Like the Israelites entering the promised land, you too, at this very moment, are standing in the middle of a story unfolding. And the story is not over.

What powers our perseverance through the ever-changing circumstances of life is the never-changing presence of God. His goodness towards every one of his children clothes every second of every single season they will ever inhabit. Including the hard ones. In the most famous psalm of all, Psalm 23, David acknowledges that the Lord leads him through seasons that feel like pleasant green pastures and restorative still waters (v 2-3) as well as seasons that can only be described as "the valley of the shadow of death" (v 4). Yet he is so convinced of God's unchanging goodness toward him that he still exclaims in verse 6, "Surely goodness and mercy will follow me all the days of my life"!

David knew that while the seasons change, God does not. He is "the Father of lights, with whom there is no variation or shadow due to change" (James 1:17). He is the Saviour who "is the same yesterday and today and for ever" (Hebrews 13:8). When we accept our present season, along with the joys and challenges and limitations that come with it, we'll discover that we're actually not missing out at all. We'll discover gratitude for what is behind us, hope for what is ahead of us, and joy in the season that God has right now set before us. You need not fear the changes that come with time when you are banking all that you are on the God who is constant. For if God is sovereign over the seasons of your life, then you can trust him in every season of that life.

CHAPTER FOUR

LULLS
Waiting Times

"Waiting is a period of learning. The longer we wait, the more we hear about him for whom we are waiting. Waiting is not a static state, it is a time when God is working behind the scenes, and the primary focus of His work is on us."

HENRI NOUWEN

Have you ever experienced the strange sensation of time slowing down? It's quite surreal. Seconds, usually so predictably consistent, are elongated into hours, and clumps of days stretch out into what feels like decades. There are at least three situations that, when intensified, have the capacity to lead us into such distorted experiences of time.

The first is bliss. Those prolonged, rapturous moments of *kairos* time when the dial of delight is turned up to maximum volume and we are so felicitously tuned in to the goodness of the present that we forget about time all together. Usually such bliss coincides with mountaintop moments of love: being overwhelmed with a sense of God's presence in worship; or the first kiss of true love; or cradling your first child as their cries yield to the unsure "sh-sh-sh" of your voice and they relax into the security of your arms and you can barely believe that love of this kind is even possible. Sacred seconds, when the march of *chronos* slows down to the pace of one who wades through chest-deep water—and like water, time seems to swirl around us rather than whoosh past us.

The second is danger. Time has a way of slowing down not only when life is full but when life is on the line. Danger expands our experience of the seconds that tick past when our adrenaline rises. Those who have lived through a serious car crash or who've engaged in military combat can attest to the sensation of slowness that comes in such moments.

But for most of us, the most common occasion that brings time to a standstill is this third one: waiting. And maybe that's because waiting—unlike peaks of bliss or valleys of danger—makes up so much of the rest of life. Like waiting for our name to be called for an appointment or for traffic to clear up so we can get to where we need to be. Or like a toddler watching the unbearably slow countdown of a microwave to announce the readiness of a snack. Perhaps you can relate to the following reflection from my friend, Laura Haas:

> It's yet another one of those days where I feel like Time barged in, unannounced. Uninvited. Unrestrained. Taking, taking, taking all the time. … My daughter waits with me, watching the numbers count down, waiting for her snack. She winces and throws her head back: "Ma-". The first syllable is clipped, engulfed by exasperation. She whimpers then sharply inhales. The last syllable is drawn out, "-maaaa!" The contrast reminds me that time is both hurried and elongated. The irony is not lost on me; an appliance designed for the instantaneous, taking far too long. How do I introduce a two-year-old to Time?[15]

And then there is the harder kind of waiting. Like waiting to regain your health from serious illness or for chronic pain to go away or for a prodigal child to finally come home. And in such moments, time often seems to play a cruel trick on us in allowing us to feel the full duration of every millisecond in which we don't yet possess what we deeply desire.

The experience of waiting is encountered in varying degrees and goes by many other names. Anticipation. Boredom. Expectation. It's the longing for something to begin that hasn't yet arrived. Times that feel like between-times. Seasons that seem out of season. Days in which we acutely feel the sharp edge of the proverb, "Hope deferred makes the heart sick, but a desire fulfilled is a tree of life" (Proverbs 13:12). And here we discover a thread woven into each of these three time-slowing experiences. They all have to do with hope.

In bliss, we hope it won't end.

In danger, we hope it will end.

But in waiting, we just *hope*.

And that's what makes waiting so hard. It's the "in-betweenness" that is so insufferable. The present stillness mingled with future possibility. Like a surfer looking out to the horizon, hoping to catch a glimpse of swell that will rise to form the next wave to ride, so too are we who live on this side of prayers yet unanswered and dreams yet unrealised. And so we wait. And we wait. And we wait.

How do we wait well? How do we grow in hope instead of anxiously wringing our hands with worry or despair? How do we not waste our waiting, since waiting makes up so much of living?

We remember that God stands sovereign not only over our appointed times but our in-between times.

GOD OF THE IN-BETWEEN TIMES

Hope, by its very definition, is a future-oriented sensation that is felt acutely in the present. It implies an unrealised yet longed-for reality. Paul says as much in Romans 8:24-25, writing, "Now hope that is seen is not hope. For who hopes for what he sees? But if we hope for what we do not see, we wait for it with patience." Later in that same letter, he goes on to describe God as "the God of hope" and prays that he will "fill you with all joy and peace in believing, so that by the power of the Holy Spirit you may abound in hope" (Romans 15:13). If God is the "God of hope", who desires that his people would "abound in hope", then we need not be troubled by extended periods of time in our lives—difficult as they may be—when we learn the important lessons that hope teaches us.

For our God not only meets us on the mountaintops and sustains us in the valleys; he is the God of the in-between: of those unspectacular rolling hills that fill the space between where we are and mountains on the horizon where we want to be. Like the lulls between waves or the white space between lines on the pages of this book, these seemingly uneventful stretches of your life between the moments that make up the highlight reel of your Instagram feed belong to God too. They may be ordinary and unmemorable, yet they are God-created and good. In fact, they are the very seasons when he does some of his most important work in you.

Just take an honest look at the Scriptures. Those who knew God deeply and loved God greatly, through whom God was pleased to do his mightiest works, didn't experience the spectacular on a daily basis. Actually, much of their lives looked just like yours and mine, as they too learned what it meant to be faithfully present on those long plateaus of human normality.

Think of Joseph, to whom God gave a specific promise in a dream, and who then waited for 14 years for the fulfilment of that promise—navigating a series of betrayals and disappointments (along with extended time in an Egyptian prison) to prepare him for that day.

Or Moses, who led millions of God's people out of slavery into freedom. But before he did, God hid him away for 40 years in the desert, shaping him and preparing him for the appointed time.

Or David, the one that God told the prophet Samuel to anoint as king, who then spent the next 15 years of his life faithfully tending his flocks in the silence of obscurity; faithfully serving the then king, Saul; or hiding in caves when Saul kept changing his mind about whether he wanted David around or wanted David dead. And David patiently waited to ascend to the throne he was anointed for—he refused to hurry God's timing by taking the life of the king who was seeking to take his.

And then there is Paul: he who humbly lamented himself as "the least of the apostles" (1 Corinthians 15:8-9), whose ministry unquestionably had the greatest impact on the church out of all the apostles. Paul's conversion from persecutor to believer was dramatic and instant, and he immediately went public as a bold witness for Jesus, to the point that his former comrades were plotting his assassination (see Acts 9). But we often forget that he was then sent away into the deserts of Arabia (Galatians 1:17-18), where he spent the next three years relearning what he knew about God in light of his encounter with the risen Christ. And it wouldn't be until another nine to ten years later—time spent quietly but faithfully serving Jesus in unrecorded ways back in his hometown of Tarsus—that he would be invited by Barnabas to minister with him in Antioch (Acts 11:25-26).

Think about that for a moment. The most influential voice in Christianity other than Jesus—the multilingual genius who authored roughly two thirds of the New Testament—was hidden away in Arabian anonymity, being prepared for the appointed time of great fruitfulness in his public ministry. There may not have been a lot happening around Paul during these hidden years of waiting. But without a doubt, there was much happening in Paul preparing him for the time ahead of him.

And so it is with us. God uses the times between what we think should be "our times" to prepare us for his appointed times. He is at work in the waiting. He has purposed those times when it seems like months are contained within a day and when lifetimes are lived within a month, to deepen in us two vital expressions of our creatureliness: our praying and our trusting.

LEARNING TO PRAY, LEARNING TO TRUST

After talking about hope and waiting in Romans 8:25, Paul goes on to say, "Likewise the Spirit helps us in our weakness. For we do not know what to pray for as we ought" (v 26). Notice what Paul does not say. He doesn't say that the Spirit helps us in our *weaknesses* (plural) but in our "weakness" (singular). In other words, weakness is not a negative condition that you and I sometimes lapse into when we're not operating in the sweet spot of our strengths. Weakness is what we *are*. Paul is reminding us of our humanity: that we live within time as those who must wait and hope and depend and pray.

All human prayer is an acknowledgement of weakness. It is the vocalised Godward expression of those who hope. Prayer is the finite calling on the infinite, the limited leaning on the limitless, the insufficient drawing upon the all-sufficient Saviour, who said, "My grace is sufficient for you" (2 Corinthians 12:9). And in this way, prayer becomes to us a weapon through which we slay the soul-corrupting, Satan-produced pride of self-reliance. I once heard my friend Ray Ortlund say that "prayer is not an option for the spiritually elite; prayer is oxygen for exhausted sinners and failures". In other words, prayer is to the waiting person what air is to the drowning person. How can we think that our waiting is wasted if, in our waiting, we are learning to pray?

I think of Adoniram Judson, the first missionary to Burma, who spent his first seven years there without a single person coming to faith in Jesus. But in the lull of his waiting, as he continued to seed the soil of Burmese hearts with the gospel, he watered those seeds with the tears of his prayers. He was a man of much prayer because he believed with all his heart, as he is often quoted as saying, that "the future is as bright as the promises of God". That God sovereignly moved at his own divine pace. And for almost seven years it appeared that nothing was happening.

But then the first Burmese person in history turned to Jesus. A few months later, a couple more followed.

By the end of Judson's life, 38 years after arriving on the shores of Burma, there were over 7,000 men and women following Jesus in Burma. And a 2020 census revealed that there are now over three million professing believers in that country. To Judson, those early decades may have seemed like little more than sowing, suffering, praying and waiting. But it was in the lulls—those times of stillness before the next set of waves rolled in, those seasons of persistent prayer when no fruit had yet blossomed on the vine, no crop had yet sprouted on the ground, and all seemed stationary and quiet—that God was at work.

The lulls of life teach us "to pray and not lose heart" (Luke 18:1). And as we learn to pray, we also learn to trust. For we soon realise that prayer is not an enchanted lamp through which we magically get what *we* want whenever we want it; but it is instead the divinely appointed means through which God will accomplish what *he* wants, both in our lives and in this world. And when there is a delay between our requests and God's answers, when seasons of suffering run longer than what we think we can bear, in those times God enlarges our capacity to trust.

GIVING GOD OUR WAITING

That doesn't make waiting easy. But it does mean that our

waiting isn't wasted. We are learning, one slow day at a time, to exhale the longings of our hope onto God and to inhale the invincible certainty of his promise to work all things together for our good (Romans 8:28). Why can we be certain of this? Because our hope is not mere optimism for a potentially brighter future; it is grounded in the definite and sure past work of Jesus. Make no mistake: Christian hope is not about potential but about promised reality, secured through the blood of Jesus and sealed with his resurrection.

In Laura's example of learning to wait with a two-year-old while a microwave counts down, she asks and answers the question for all of those who are learning to live in the in-between:

> How do I live faithfully between the Now and the Not Yet? How do I most beautifully decorate the present space between Time Past and Eternity Future? Each passing second with my daughter in that kitchen reminds me that there is coming a Day when Time will be taken away. That at the crescendo of creation, Time as we know it will take a bow as Eternity dances her way onto the stage. And yet, these short days have meaning beyond the reach of Time.

> "I'm proud of the way you are waiting" I whisper softly, as much to my own heart as to my daughter. Then I offer my waiting to the One who exists outside of Time. The One for whom Time is just a wristwatch, soon to be taken off and laid on a cosmic dresser. I decide that, one day, that's what I'll tell [my daughter] about Time: how to receive it as a gift from the Author of it, and how to offer it all back to Him, the only One not restrained by it. For He alone exists not only within Time, but eternally before it, ever ahead of it, and sovereignly above it. Remembering that, is my pathway to living

faithfully between the here-and-now and the one-day-when.[16]

There are deep truths to drink of even while waiting for the microwave. So do not despise the slow times soaked with routine and ordinariness. God is in those times. And while it may not seem like a lot of great things are happening around you, there is a great thing happening in you. God is not behind schedule in your life because your life is happening on his schedule. In the waiting, you are learning to be human. You are learning to embrace your humanity rather than always trying to rid yourself of it. You are learning to wait, but to wait with hope. To suffer, but to suffer well. To pray, but to pray with a persevering anticipation. But above all, you are learning to trust.

CHAPTER FIVE

HURRY
Never Enough Time

*"The solution to an overbusy life is not more time. It's to slow
down and simplify our lives around what really matters."*
JOHN MARK COMER

I was crying on an airplane, and it honestly wasn't my
fault. I wasn't ready. As I sat there in my seat, deprived of
sleep on a 14-hour flight, watching the beginning of what I
thought would be a light-hearted movie to help me nod off, I
was emotionally ambushed. The culprit? The Pixar movie *Up*.
This seemingly innocuous film for children grabbed hold of
my heartstrings and pulled until the tears came.

In what is arguably one of the most moving opening
sequences of any film, *Up* shows a young boy named Carl, who
falls in love and eventually marries his childhood sweetheart,
Ellie. Together they dream of becoming adventurers in
Venezuela, with Carl vowing to get them there someday.
But life keeps getting in the way, and so they ride the highs
and lows together until the sequence concludes with Carl's
beloved Ellie falling sick in old age and passing away, and Carl
then living alone as a grumpy old man, angry at the world,
haunted by his own unfulfilled promises.

And yes, that's all in the first ten minutes. Of a children's
movie.

But this surprisingly deep movie presses a universal cliché into our hearts: *time flies*.

MAXIMISING OUR TIME, BUT MISSING THE POINT

As we saw in the previous chapter, there are occasions in our life—particularly when we're waiting—when time seems to drag its feet and pass us by painfully slowly. Yet the opposite is also true. Time also moves fast—sometimes at lightning speed. Which is why we say things like "Time is of the essence", "Time waits for no one", and "Where did the time go?" Since time is precious and limited, we hunt for best practices through which we can *save* time and avoid situations in which we feel like we are *wasting* time. We look back on a special day or a vacation or even entire decades of life with disbelief at how quickly they slipped from the horizon of our windscreen into the rear-view mirror. Before we knew it, dreams were fossilised into memories. And the older we get, the faster that horizon seems to approach. The Russian poet Anna Akhmatova pointed out that wars and plagues all eventually pass by, "but which of us can cope with … the terror that is named the flight of time?"[17]

How do we typically respond to time's flight? We hurry. Like ~~my beloved wife~~ a hypothetical person trying to fit their every possession into a suitcase for a week-long trip, many of us try to cram everything we possibly can into our short lives. After all, we want our limited number of days on this earth to count for something, right? But before long, we hear ourselves answering the question of "Hey, how've you been?" with the increasingly predictable response of "Busy!"—as if busyness is synonymous with righteousness. As if the output of *our* work is what justifies us. Like Esau trading his birthright for a bowl of stew, we exchange faithful presence for perpetual busyness. Then we repeat this cycle day after day after day, wondering when we're going to finally find some time—wondering why our lives can be so full and yet simultaneously feel so empty?

Why are we in such a hurry?

Don't get me wrong: I'm all for efficiency and an unwasted life. There is a time to move fast, particularly in time-sensitive circumstances and crisis situations. Neither laziness nor apathy have any place within the Christian life. But here's a hard truth we need to face: *doing more does not mean we are doing well.* Not all of life is a crisis, requiring our hurry. And when we constantly live that way, we start missing life. Like riding a motorcycle with no eye-protection, where the speed of our movement forces our eyes to squint and wind-induced tears blur our vision, so too is a life of perpetual hurry. We stop noticing things; each week becomes a blur.

What does it profit us to rush through life toward our final years, ever hurrying to arrive at the next thing, only to miss the main things: being faithfully present to God, and to the good works he has prepared for us to walk in, woven into each day we wake up in (Ephesians 2:10)? What does it profit to achieve much but lose those we love along the way? To gain the world but lose our very selves (Luke 9:25)?

Despite all the technological upgrades over this past century that purport to save us time—from cooking fires to air-fryers, horses to cars, wooden ships to airplanes, handwriting to typing, letters to emails, and countless more—we all feel the unsettling disquiet of having less time than ever. Why is that? It's not that each of these upgrades don't free up more minutes in each of our day. They most certainly do. Our problem is that we keep raising the bar. We keep filling those new minutes gained with an expectation of greater productivity. And even when we do find a little space to think, our thoughts tend to drift toward that which still needs to be *done*—the next bill to pay or project to finish or week to plan. Far from living fully alive to God and others and ourselves, we are depleted of life: often so exhausted that we finish each day trying to escape our life with a few hours of binge-watching another show or doom-scrolling online. And we wonder why we're tired and anxious and frustrated by never having enough time?

There is a better way.

LEARNING TO STROLL IN A HURRIED WORLD

The answer is not to try to find more time. You have the same weekly 168 hours as Jesus and every other person who ever walked the earth. The answer is to give ourselves to the countercultural rhythm of *walking* with Jesus—which, at the risk of stating the obvious, is something that happens at a slower pace. Walking pace. Have you ever considered that the pace of faithfulness is probably slower than you might expect? The verb used most frequently for being faithfully present to God and his purposes throughout the Scriptures is that of walking. In the Old Testament, Moses reminds us that "Enoch walked with God" (Genesis 5:24) and "Noah walked with God" (Genesis 6:9), and he instructs God's people to "walk in all the way that the LORD your God has commanded you, that you may live, and that it may go well with you" (Deuteronomy 5:33).

In the New Testament, the apostle Paul does likewise, reminding us that sanctification happens at walking pace as we "walk by the Spirit" (Galatians 5:16) and "keep in step with the Spirit" (v 25). In fact, hundreds of times in the Bible, faithfulness to God and our relationship with God are described as a *walk*. Only six times is the comparison with a *run* or a *race* (1 Corinthians 9:24-26; Galatians 2:2; 5:7; Philippians 2:16; 2 Timothy 4:7; Hebrews 12:1). And even then, the context of almost all of those passages is that of a "finish line" or a "prize". Christianity is compared to *running* when God wants us to think about endurance and perseverance. The point is not so much speed but a steadfast single-mindedness toward a destination.

Consider the tension in Ephesians 5:15-16, when Paul writes, "Look carefully then how you walk, not as unwise but as wise, making the best use of the time, because the days are evil". In verse 16, Paul commands us to make the most of the time we have. But in verse 15, he describes the Christian life as a *walk*. So "making the best use of the time" cannot mean living in a rush or being forever busy. Moral or missional urgency—the context in which Paul's instructions appear—should never be confused with hurry.

Living faithfully present to God and others means we are to "walk in love, as Christ loved us" (v 2). And do you remember the first quality of this Christ-like love, according to Paul, in his famous chapter on love in 1 Corinthians 13? "Love is patient" (v 4). What if our urgency for those around us to know the love of Christ were matched with the kind of patience that Jesus has shown to us? Authentic Christianity happens more slowly than we think, which means being patient with others—as well as ourselves—and committing to moving at the pace of love.

And this pace is to permeate into every area of our lives. What if we were to allow ourselves actual margin in our days for unhurried delight in the life we have? To make it a point to watch the sun come up or go down and admire the unique colours that God paints the sky with that day... To allocate time for cultivating wonder, reading widely, and thinking deeply... To have bandwidth in our days to walk and be attentive and receive without frustration the providential interruptions that God sends our way. After all, Jesus doesn't want your busyness. He wants your fruitfulness (John 15:5, 16). And fruit can't be hurried. Fruit happens slowly, as we abide in him.

JESUS WANTS YOUR ATTENTION, NOT YOUR BUSYNESS

I love the way John Mark Comer phrases the question in his book *The Ruthless Elimination of Hurry*: "The central question of our apprenticeship to Jesus is pretty straightforward: How would Jesus live if he were me?"[18] Take a moment to remember that old WWJD (What Would Jesus Do?) wristband you might have been given at a youth camp back in your ancient past, and seriously consider this: *How would Jesus live if he were me? In my job? In my home? With my neighbours? With my present responsibilities and commitments?*

Here's one thing I can guarantee you: if Jesus were living my life, he wouldn't be as hurried as I am. In fact, he wouldn't be hurried at all. In fact, through every event and season of Jesus' life in the Gospels, never once is he in a hurry. And Jesus does not want our hurried busyness, even when it's busyness for him. In Luke 10:38-42, when Martha welcomed Jesus into her house, she got busy serving and preparing food. Meanwhile, her sister Mary sat at Jesus' feet and listened to his teaching.

> *But Martha was distracted with much serving. And she went up to him and said, "Lord, do you not care that my sister has left me to serve alone? Tell her then to help me." But the Lord answered her, "Martha, Martha, you are anxious and troubled about many things, but one thing is necessary. Mary has chosen the good portion, which will not be taken away from her. (v 40-42)*

The issue was not that Martha was serving but that she had become distracted in her serving. Her busyness made her present work the focus, rather than the presence of Jesus the focus. She had missed the point. And when we believe the most important thing in the room is *what* we're doing rather than *who* we're with—and *Who* is with us—we, too, miss the point. And our entitlement growls, hungering for recognition or demanding that others join us in our busyness.

And Jesus wants us to repent.

To repent of living hurried, at the speed of the world instead of the pace of the Spirit.

To repent of living busy, ever seeking to cram one more thing in because we fear missing out.

To repent of being so ruled by our to-do lists that we have turned into lousy friends.

To repent of living over-scheduled, allowing everyone *except Jesus* to set our calendar or define what fullness is.

To repent of living distracted, missing the life we have before us because we have been seduced by the siren song of worldly success, which promises satisfaction but will only devour us.

To repent of our delusions of omnipresence, which have us so glued to our screens that we forget to look into the eyes of those around us.

Perhaps you're wondering where we might begin to pump the brakes on our constant rush toward the future? We'll think more about this in the next chapter. But we can start by eliminating the word "busy" as an adjective for our Christian lives. Let's admit that the root of our busyness is deeper than having just having too much to do. It's that we are refusing to be fully human: refusing to acknowledge our limitedness by thinking that we can live well at a pace that was faster than that of Jesus. Have you ever considered that Jesus knew the future and still was never in a hurry to get there? Instead, he trusted the Father's timing and walked at the pace of love. That's the pace he wants us to walk at with him.

RELAX—GOD IS REIGNING IN YOUR FUTURE TOO

Underneath Martha's distracted busyness, Jesus shows us the engine that drives so much of our perpetual hurry: "You are anxious and troubled about many things" (v 41). Worry is the result of thinking that the certainty of our future, and the comfort of our present, is entirely riding on us and is at any moment about to slip away from us. So we worry about our plans for the coming years and our future security, forgetting that God's plan will prevail and that our future is resurrection. We worry that God will be disappointed with us if we fail to do this thing or that, because we think he is like us, measuring our worth by our achievements instead of what Christ has achieved for us. We worry about what people will think of us, so we fail to say "no" and schedule our lives with inhuman expectations. Our hurrying through the present is the result of our worry about our future—be that decades from now or just later this afternoon. But we need not fear what waits for us in our future. Why? Because God himself will be there.

Isn't the problem with much of our anxiety about the future that we are creating a scenario in our mind in which God is not included? That's a hypothetical impossibility—because it is a future where God has stopped being *God*. My friend Sam Allberry points out that "when we imagine all those worst-case scenarios, we are imagining them without factoring in the presence and grace of God that would be there if they actually happened … [God] only gives grace for our actual situation."[19]

Future-you will indeed face troubles that will make you anxious. But future-you will still be upheld by the faithfulness of God. So relax; God will still be God over every day ahead of you. What he wants from us now is the posture for which he commended Mary and to which he calls every one of his followers: attentiveness to him in our *today*, instead of anxiously hurrying towards tomorrow.

SLOW DOWN, RECEIVE TODAY

In his famous Sermon on the Mount, Jesus speaks directly to the anxiety that comes from obsessing over the length of our days and the all-too-real needs ahead. In Matthew 6, he commands us not to be anxious about these needs (v 25) and reminds us that even the daily needs of "the birds of the air" (v 26) and "the lilies of the field" (v 28-30) are not overlooked by the Father. Jesus asks, "And which of you by being anxious can add a single hour to his span of life?" (v 27). In other words, learn to answer your anxieties about the future with the sermon on God's faithfulness that the created world is preaching to you right now. Or, as Martin Luther, that wonderfully sarcastic 16th-century German Reformer, put it:

> It seems ... that the flowers stand there and make us blush and become our teachers. Thank you, flowers, you, who are to be devoured by the cows! God has exalted you very highly, that you become our masters and teachers![20]

Then again, in verse 34, Jesus repeats his command with further clarity: "Therefore do not be anxious about tomorrow, for tomorrow will be anxious for itself. Sufficient for the day is its own trouble." What would it look like for you to trade in your worries about the future for faithful presence in today? Jesus wants you to give yourself entirely to God's gift of today. For what is your former future, now known as your past, but the sum of your *todays*?

Today is when you will meet satisfying joys and sanctifying sorrows.

Today is filled with moments, large and small, that are loaded with *kairos*.

Today is what God graces us for, not our imaginary tomorrows.

Today is "the day that the LORD has made; let us rejoice and be glad in it" (Psalm 118:24).

Today is when God wants us to live, at rest in the promise that he himself will inhabit your tomorrows.

In Christ, the reason you need never worry about the future is because your future will never be absent of him. Instead, he promises, "I will never leave you nor forsake you" (Hebrews 13:5). So do not be anxious about tomorrow. Tomorrow belongs to God. Believing that, you can trade in your worries about the future and be faithfully present to what he places before you, today.

CHAPTER SIX

PAUSES
Resting Times

"It is easy for me to imagine that the next great division of the world will be between people who wish to live as creatures and people who wish to live as machines."
WENDELL BERRY

One of the most important skills in speaking—whether face to face or on a stage—is knowing the importance of when not to. Let's call it the art of pausing. The difference between a powerful sentence and mere noise, or between a joke that hits home and one that flies over people's heads, often comes down to the use of a *pause*: an intentional space between words that gives weight to the message of those words.

Have you ever been in a conversation with someone who *really* likes to talk? You know who I'm talking about. The kind of person who enjoys talking so much that they don't ever seem to stop. Those whose lips spill words like a waterfall spills the river: *unceasingly*. No breaks. No full stops or periods. There are barely even commas. Just an ever-flowing sequence of sounds until you either interject or they are called away. The extroverts find themselves a little frustrated by such people because they can barely get a word in. The introverts find themselves mildly mortified, perhaps tuning out ever so slightly and subconsciously wondering, "When did they last take a breath? Are they going to stop? Is God punishing me?!"

An inability to stop talking could stem from the pride of never wanting to listen to others; or perhaps it's more of a naive carelessness that simply lacks self-awareness; or maybe it's nervousness, because, to some of us, silence feels awkward and scary. Whatever the reason, the absence of pauses reveals an overestimation of the importance of a person's own voice. Without pauses, our words blur together into a long, dull drone.

And what an unceasing talker sounds like, an unceasing doer looks like. Always producing, always working, always doing, always planning, always moving—a person for whom busyness is a drug and productivity is lord.

YOU ARE NOT A MACHINE

The world you and I inhabit is a world of noise and speed and sweat, ruled by a tyrant named *Productivity*. The god of *Productivity* weighs us with the measure of our last performance; you are no more than the sum of what you produce. Yet when our value is tied to our output, to stop producing means to stop mattering. Perhaps that's why stillness feels so alien to us. But, like all idols, regardless of what *Productivity* promises, it will demand exceedingly more than it gives. We are promised success but at the cost of our families; we are promised meaningful accomplishment but permitted no time to gratefully enjoy it; we are promised fullness of life at the expense of depleting our energy, our adrenal glands and our joy.

If we are what we do, then we must rarely be not-doing. As expectations around our output have increased, so too have expectations for our availability. The persistent pings of emails, messages, social-media interactions and news alerts from the devices in our pockets has corrupted our collective minds into believing that fullness of life is one of constant connectivity. *Write this. Like this. Click this. Engage with this. Respond to this. Notice this. Learn this.* On average, we now pick up our smartphones 81,500 times each year, or roughly once every 4.3 minutes of our waking lives.[21] And the result is that more and more people are either forgetting or refusing to disconnect. Many of us tend to believe that stopping to rest is an admission of failure. Our heart wonders, "If I'm not achieving or producing or performing… then am I failing?" But stopping to rest is not an admission of failure. It is an admission of humanity.

You are not a machine but a human. And we are each learning to be humans by learning not only what God has called us to do but also what he has called us to not do. I am not unlimited, so I need to prioritise rest. I am not omnipotent, so I need to prioritise prayer. I am not omniscient, so I need to learn to listen. I am not omnipresent, so I need to stop trying to be everywhere for everyone and instead become comfortable with rhythms indispensable to healthy humanity.

What I want you to see over the next couple of pages is that when it comes to our activity, the ability to pause, to cease, to simply *be*, is a mark of humility because it acknowledges the limitations that God has woven into our humanity. It is in this way that pausing is a mark of maturity. When we were young, we never wanted to stop—which is why bedtime with small children so frequently feels like battling a mythological Hydra; one child is successfully put down, but two more rise up to take their place. For children often see the pause of rest as missing out—as wasted time.

But pausing when God calls us to pause is never wasted time.

It is in the stopping—the pauses between our words—that our voices gain impact.

It is in the stopping—the pauses between our work—that our lives gain impact.

For it is in our pauses that we acknowledge that our time belongs to God. So, in this chapter, we're going to consider how to hit pause—daily, weekly, and strategically because it is in our pauses that we not only demonstrate humility but further learn its wisdom.

SELAH: PAUSING EACH DAY

One word found frequently throughout the Psalms—71 times, in fact—is a Hebrew word that, ironically, we often skim past: *selah*. It's ironic because this word is an instruction that likely means "pause and reflect".

Selah.

Slow down, and consider what you have just heard or prayed or sung or read.

Selah.

Stop speaking and be still.

Psalm 46 begins with humanity confessing our need and ends with God commanding our attention:

> *Be still, and know that I am God.*
>   *I will be exalted among the nations,*
>   *I will be exalted in the earth!"*
> *The LORD of hosts is with us;*
>   *the God of Jacob is our fortress. Selah (v 10-11)*

To be still before the Lord in a world of unceasing words and unending work is an act of daily worship: a God-exalting counterrevolution against a self-absorbed world. Rather than a blurred rush of minutes and hours, what if your day was marked with pauses that helped you to behold God? What if you took these comforting words of the "Godness" of God— "Be still, and know that I am God"—and turned them into a keystone habit that gives shape to your day?

Here's what that could look like. When you rise in the morning, take a moment to pause and remember that God is God over everything that comes your way in the hours ahead. Then punctuate the day ahead with brief moments of *selah*. As the morning closes and you break for lunch, and as the afternoon finishes and you prepare for the evening, pause and look back over the hours that have passed, entrusting them into God's hands.

Practically, I've found that putting a reminder into my phone at the end of the morning and afternoon blocks of the day (11:50 a.m. and 5:50 p.m.) has helped me to look away from my work and just be still before the Lord: to rest in his presence, to confess sin, to ask for help, to be grateful, and to exhale my cares onto him because he cares for me (1 Peter 5:7).

Then, at the end of each day, practise the worshipful pause of laying your head down onto your pillow. Did you realise that even your sleeping is an act of worship? In your sleeping you acknowledge that because God is wide awake as the Sustainer of this world, you can close your eyes. Author Tish Harrison Warren writes:

> What if Christians were known as a countercultural community of the well-rested—people who embrace our limits with zest and even joy? ... About one third of our lives are spent in sleep. Through these collective years of rest, God is at work in us and in the world, redeeming, healing, and giving grace. Each night when we yield to sleep, we practice letting go of our reliance on self-effort and abiding in the good grace of our Creator.[22]

Every day of our lives, multiple times each day, we need to reclaim the practice of pausing our work and silencing the noise to rehearse these words to our own hearts: "Be still, and know that I am God".

SABBATH: A WEEKLY SANCTUARY IN TIME

The word Sabbath comes from a Hebrew word that literally means "to cease" or "to rest". The Scriptures teach that after creating the universe as we know it, "on the seventh day God finished his work that he had done, and he rested on the seventh day from all his work that he had done. So God blessed the seventh day and made it holy" (Genesis 2:2-3). Have you ever considered that the very first thing in Scripture that God himself set apart as holy was not an object or a place but a period of time?

It was this act of God at creation that later set the pattern for the Jewish Sabbath—a weekly day of rest commanded for all God's people (Exodus 20:8-11). While the practice of Sabbath as it was for the Israelites is no longer required of New Testament Christians, the principle undergirding it remains. God has built a rhythm into existence for the sake of human flourishing, in which, every seven days, we pause from efforts to produce, and we practise worshipful gratitude for what we have. Eugene Peterson reminds us that it is "not a day to get anything done but a day to watch and be responsive to what God has done".[23] A day that reminds of us of our humanity—that being faithfully present means embracing our limits and being aware of our need to rest.

Life may indeed be a struggle, but it is also a gift. Jesus taught us to view the Sabbath in this way—as God's gift to us—when he said, "The Sabbath was made for man, not man for the Sabbath. So the Son of Man is lord even of the Sabbath" (Mark 2:27-28). To refuse such a gracious gift only reveals that we treat our work with more seriousness than God's word. Like a joke without a pause is a life without a regular Sabbath; it just doesn't land.

I love the way that Abraham Heschel describes the Sabbath as a "sanctuary in time".[24] A sanctuary is a place of refuge and renewal. A sanctuary within time is a period of renewal, carved into each week, when we can breathe again: inhaling God's unwavering faithfulness and exhaling all that burdens us into his care.

The Sabbath is a sanctuary in time, in which time is sanctified—that is, set apart—for the explicit purpose of practising delight in both the Creator and what he has created. It is when we remember that the sum of our life is not in what we accumulate or achieve but in what we have been given. It is a 24-hour period located within each week of our lives that reminds us that whatever amount of time has been allotted to us is precious, that life is a gift, and that we are first and foremost worshippers rather than workers. As Heschel describes it, this sanctuary within time called "Sabbath" is "a realm of time where the goal is not to have but to be, not to own but to give, not to control but to share, not to subdue but to be in accord".[25]

If all this is sounding a long way from your current weekly routine and you're wondering where to begin, I've been greatly helped by author Pete Scazzero's four easy-to-remember statements. Each Sabbath, you're essentially looking to do four things. *Stop work. Enjoy rest. Practise delight. Contemplate God.*[26]

1. *Stop work*: What do I need to pause? What areas of productivity—both paid and unpaid—need to cease as an act of worshipful trust in God?

2. *Enjoy rest*: What fills my tank? How can I make space to do some of those things as part of my Sabbath?

3. *Practise delight*: What parts of God's creation bring me joy? What sights, sounds, tastes, places and friendships reveal God's goodness and deepen my delight?

4. *Contemplate God*: Where have I seen God's sovereignty, goodness and grace in my life in this past week, which I need to consciously bring to mind? As I open my Bible and gather with other believers to behold God, what about him is worthy of my worship?

In this light, the Sabbath is not so much a break from life; it's the point of life—the pinnacle of life! It is a foretaste of the new creation—a weekly sip of the world to come. Have you ever considered the Sabbath in *that* light? As a recurring preview of your future, experienced in the present? What could be more important (and life-renewing!) than setting apart a day each week to experience *that*?

SOLITUDE: STRATEGIC WITHDRAWAL, LIKE JESUS

Finally, there will be times when the circumstances of our life will require us to step back from our regular schedule and pause more strategically.

While community with others is vital, not all of life is communal. The spiritual discipline of solitude is how we press pause on community and service to others in order to be attentive to God. How easily we forget that even Jesus— the perfect human—would frequently leave the crowds, his ministry responsibilities and the demands of the eternally important work he had come to do in order to be alone with the Father in prayer. Matthew 14:13 records Jesus withdrawing from the crowds "to a desolate place by himself". John 6:15 tells us that "Jesus withdrew again to the mountain by himself". And Luke 5:16 shows us that these were not isolated incidents in the life of Jesus but a pattern: he often withdrew to deserted places and prayed.

Let's be honest: do we really believe that *we* are *less* in need of time in prayer than Jesus? How can we think that strategically withdrawing, like Jesus, from the demands of life to experience solitude with God is anything but an essential use of our limited time? Mike Cosper writes, "Solitude isn't an end in itself. It's rather like one half of a breath. It's the inhale, and life in community, life among our family, neighbours, coworkers, and friends, is the exhale."[27]

How these intentional breaks from normality look will vary

from person to person. You may not be able to withdraw up to a literal mountain like Jesus did. I'm thinking particularly of those who are parents in the season of life when their children are still young, or those living in shared accommodation where every room is constantly populated with others. What I want you to see is not so much the exact structure of strategic withdrawal but the importance of the principle that we *do* participate in such pauses ourselves.

Susannah Wesley—the mother of the great preaching and hymn-writing duo of the 18th century, John and Charles Wesley—had other children besides her two most famous sons. A lot of other children actually: ten in total who survived past infancy. As you can probably imagine, living in a small English home with ten children didn't quite lend itself to a restful environment or the ability to withdraw to a quiet place to be alone with Jesus. Yet she did what she could, with what she had, and came up with a creative way to withdraw into prayerful solitude.

Were you to have passed by the Wesley household and poked your head through the doorway on any given day, you might have glimpsed the curious sight of a mother sitting in her kitchen, with her long outer-apron flipped up over her head. Each of her children learned that when their mother's apron was up, she was meeting with God in quiet prayer and was not to be interrupted. There, in the midst of a bustling home of ten children, Susannah Wesley practised strategic withdrawal: resting in the Lord, in order to re-enter the fray of normal life.

GOD IS OUR REST
True rest isn't merely some time away to catch our breath or a day off or a good nap, as helpful as each of those things are. True rest is found in the worshipful posture of seeing and accepting God as *God*, and ourselves as recipients of his

strength and goodness—in seeing time as a gracious gift that he gives, not a ruthless ruler demanding we prove our worth. It's why Jesus said in Matthew 11:28, "Come to me, all of you who are weary and burdened, and I will give you rest" (CSB).

The rest we most need is far more than just the absence of work; it is time with him. Faithful presence means aligning our goals within time to God's design for time. Those spaces within time where we cease our speaking and discontinue our doing—where we reflect and receive and listen and delight in the life we have—are the God-ordained spaces where we are renewed, where God's provision is revealed, and where God is glorified as the Giver of all. And pausing from our labours to rest in him—daily, weekly, and regularly—is never time misspent.

CHAPTER SEVEN

MEMORY
Past Times

"Great is this power of memory, exceedingly great, my God—a vast and boundless chamber within me."
AUGUSTINE OF HIPPO

Memory is a curious thing. Why is it that I can remember with vibrant detail my first-grade teacher, along with the names and phone numbers of my friends in that class, but not where I put my car keys last night or the reason why I just opened a new tab in my web browser? How is it that I can remember the name of the patient snowboard instructor who helped me navigate my first day on the slopes in Loveland, Colorado as an eleven-year-old—persevering with me on the emotional journey from "I hate this and the entire concept of existence" to "This is the best day of my life!" (thank you, Albert)—but not the name of that one guy I've met and spoken with at church at least a half dozen times over the past few months, including last Sunday? And with all the responsibilities, projects and deadlines I have right now, why on earth did I wake up this morning hearing the theme song to *The Flintstones* echoing between my ears—with perfect recall of every lyric—when I haven't crossed paths with that show since the early 1990s? Memory is a curious thing.

Yet memory is a powerful thing. One of the early church fathers, Augustine, described our memory as a vast palace where the ideas, thoughts and experiences of our past are stored. In the act of remembering, some memories "are forthcoming immediately; others take longer, as if they had to be brought from some more secret place of storage".[28]And then there are other memories that we wish we could be rid of. Files in our mind that we long to delete permanently. Memories that we long to disremember, that rush into our consciousness when something in the present triggers us to re-experience trauma or failure or sin from our past. The power of memories—both those that delight us and those that cause us to shudder—is in their ability to command our attention in the here and now. According to Augustine, *memory* is our present experience of the past.[29]

Let me show you what he means.

THE RE-ANIMATING POWER OF MEMORY

Take a moment to remember the front entrance to the last place you lived in—not your present home but the one before. Can you see it? As you walk through the front entrance, navigate your way toward the kitchen. Notice the various rooms and wall-colours and various pieces of furniture you pass along the way. Now go and sit down in your favourite chair in that home and take a 360-degree look at your surroundings.

I'll give you a few moments to visualise all of that.

Now dig a little deeper. Which people from that season of your life can you picture sitting in those chairs with you? What special or difficult or hilarious moments come to mind that took place with them there?

You see, your memory brought those files of your past back to life in your present—what happened *then* makes you feel something *now*. Memories reanimate the past. Most of the time, our memories are operating just beneath the surface of our consciousness, directing the decisions we make, the habits we've formed and the skills we now possess. For example, when a potential employer looks at the experience listed on your résumé, what they are really looking at is the strength of your memory when it comes to recalling and detailing a specific skill required for the role. Again, memory is a powerful thing.

In fact, Augustine viewed our memory as fundamental to our very identity: the link between our past experiences and our present consciousness. For it is "in the chamber of my memory ... [that] I meet and remember *myself*".[30] That is, our memories make us who we are, by bringing who we've been into the unfolding narrative of our lives. In this way, our memories powerfully shape who we are becoming, even as they reveal in the present who we were. Our memories locate us because they reveal the real us—the story we *have* lived, not the story we *wish* we had lived.

And while our memories are vital to who we are and what we do and where we are going, they can also be destructive when given too much attention. Like countless other parts of God's creation, when our memories serve us and our affections for God, they are a tremendous gift. But the opposite is also true; when we prioritise the past over the present, we turn a good servant into an unrelenting tyrant. And that's the danger: the past has a habit of not staying, well, past. It infiltrates our present through our memories, seeking to regain the attention it once possessed.

So how we think about time-past, and how we interact with those thoughts, really matters.

There are two subtle ways in which the past tries to invade and commandeer our present. The first is *nostalgia*. The second is *regret*. Nostalgia robs our present through comparison; regret robs our present through condemnation. Nostalgia is the result of time missed; regret is the result of time misspent (or misappropriated from us). Both cause us to miss being faithfully present to the life God is giving us in the here and now.

NOSTALGIA: TIMES MISSED

The word "nostalgia" comes from two Greek words: *nostos* meaning "homecoming" and *álgos* meaning "ache". Nostalgia is an ache for a past that we felt more at home in. All of us carry a sense of nostalgia toward experiences, places, and friendships in our past that we hold dear. A song will come on that transports us back to our high-school years. A drive through our hometown sends a thousand memories rushing through our mind. It's understandable that we treasure the high points of our story, longing to have more of them. We naturally relate to Andy Bernard, lamenting in a profound moment during *The Office* (US version), "I wish there was a way to know you're in the good old days before you've actually left them".

But like a Snapchat or Instagram filter, nostalgia amplifies the colours of the past while airbrushing out its flaws. The trouble with nostalgia is that it exaggerates the beauty of the past and minimises its troubles, injustices and problems. Consider Israel's deliverance out of multigenerational slavery in Egypt. God provided miraculous guidance and reassurance of his presence through a pillar of cloud by day and a pillar of fire by night (Exodus 13). God provided them with a miraculous pathway through the Red Sea for their escape from slaughter (Exodus 14). God provided for their daily needs with water in the wilderness and heavenly bread called manna that quite literally landed fresh on their doorstep every morning (Exodus 15-16). They had constant reminders that God was with them in their present, just like he promised.

Yet before long, a grumbling rose up among the people, and some complained, "We remember the fish we ate in Egypt that cost nothing, the cucumbers, the melons, the leeks, the onions, and the garlic. But now our strength is dried up, and there is nothing at all but this manna to look at" (Numbers 11:5-6). Now, far be it from me to stand judge over a multitude of hangry Hebrews in the middle of the desert. Personally, I have never lamented the absence of—*checks notes*—fish, cucumbers, and garlic in my life. But that's the power of nostalgia. It reanimates memories to be better than they were, deceiving us with the lie that *God is holding out on us*. Their nostalgia overemphasised the taste of fish and cucumber, while reducing 430 years of brutality and suffering under Egyptian whips to a minor inconvenience. And so they grumbled, deep down believing that God was less faithful to them in their present than he had been in their past.

Are we really so different?

When our life takes a turn that causes us to grumble, when we lose a position of influence or our health or a loved one, when our present discipleship to Jesus feels tragically and frustratingly less than what it used to be, when we find ourselves in a time that feels like *the wrong time*, and we long for what we once had—don't we too have a tendency to photoshop the past into something better than it was? And by doing so, miss what God has for us in *this* season? And even if past times *were* objectively better, there's a way to grieve what we've lost without letting it hijack what God is doing in *this* time. The wisest man to live before Jesus came along, Solomon, warns us in Ecclesiastes 7:10, "Say not, 'Why were the former days better than these?' For it is not from wisdom that you ask this." Gratitude for former times honours God. But an excessive desire to go back, rather than forward, is to make an idol out of an experience.

REGRET: TIME MISSPENT

The second way in which the past tries to hijack the here and now is through regret. While nostalgia obsesses over past glories, regret obsesses over past failures. Time misspent, which has now trickled irreversibly through our fingers. It may be the regret of an opportunity missed. Like Uncle Rico, a failed football player in the film *Napoleon Dynamite*, caught up on what his life would look like *if only* "coach would have put me in fourth quarter—we would've been state champions. No doubt. No doubt in my mind. You better believe things would have been different. I would've gone pro… making millions of dollars, living in a big old mansion somewhere, you know, soaking it up in a hot tub with my soulmate…"

Or it may be the regret of a decision we made or a sin we committed—something we did that, humanly speaking, can't be undone. Many of us can remember harsh words that sprayed out of our mouth like a shotgun blast into the face of someone we loved. And as soon as they were said, we knew they could never be unsaid. "If only…" our memory laments. "If only I hadn't said that, done that, moved there, trusted them, quit then…"

Regret calls out to us from the grave of times past, demanding that we replay our worst moments and wasted seasons in hope of a different ending. Like ghosts that won't leave the place they once inhabited as living people, our regrets linger, haunting the palaces of our memories, refusing to move on or let us do likewise.

How do we stop the past from invading the present and robbing us of today? We answer both nostalgia and regret with the gospel. We point our nostalgic desires forward (rather than backward), to the future Christ has secured for us; and we send our every regret of sin, guilt, shame, and condemnation back to the cross, where the voice of Jesus drowns out the taunts of our accuser.

HOW THE GOSPEL REDIRECTS OUR NOSTALGIA

Gratitude, not grumbling, is the right response to good times that have faded into the rear-view mirror of our memories.

But we also need to remember that our desire for the good old days is a misdirected desire. The longings we are pointing back to times now behind us, God intends to satisfy in time yet ahead of us. We're looking in the wrong direction; true and lasting glory is in our future because our future in Christ is "an inheritance that is imperishable, undefiled, and unfading, kept in heaven for you" (1 Peter 1:4). We're not meant to obsess over the life we lived in years gone by, but to look instead to the eternal life that Christ alone has given us. No wonder Paul tells us repeatedly to fix our gaze there! He says in Colossians 3:2-4:

> *Set your minds on things that are above, not on things that are on earth. For you have died, and your life is hidden with Christ in God. When Christ who is your life appears, then you also will appear with him in glory.*

How easily we forget that the highest pinnacles of bliss in this life are merely the baseline for the world to come. The goodness of past times is put into perspective when we remember that every delight we experience now is merely a foretaste of the feast that is on the way. No matter how good your glory days *were*, in Christ your real glory days are still *yet to be*.

While remembrance of our past is helpful for stoking the fires of prayer and hope, we must refuse to allow it to rule in our hearts today. In the same way that God did not design your body to be sustained today by a meal you had back in 2015, neither does he intend to nourish your soul with the provisions of grace he granted you in the past.

No—he wants to give you grace *today*. He desires that you come to him *today*. To worship him *today*. To ask for his provision *today*. To trust that he is good and that he does good (Psalm 119:68) *today*. The God of infinite power and wisdom and goodness and glory will not fail to satisfy those who seek him. We just need to make sure that we're looking in the right place. C.S Lewis reminds us:

> On every level of our life … we are always harking back to some occasion which seemed to us to reach perfection, setting that up as a norm and depreciating all other occasions by comparison. But these other occasions, I now suspect, are often full of their own new blessings if only we would lay ourselves open to it. God shows us a new facet of the glory, and we refuse to look at it because we're still looking for the old one … And the joke, or tragedy of it all is that these golden moments in the past, which are so tormenting if we erect them into a norm, are entirely nourishing, wholesome, and enchanting if we are content to accept them for what they are, for memories.[31]

HOW THE GOSPEL CONQUERS OUR REGRETS

Perhaps you have a tendency to self-flagellation, constantly revisiting the scenes of failure in your past. It need not even be the failures of your youth; many of us get trapped in a vicious cycle of self-loathing by simply replaying the failures of this past week. Satan is the accuser, who taunts us with our very real sins—and sometimes the sins of others that he'd like us to blame on ourselves. He mocks, "You've been following Jesus for how long now, and you *still* can't get it right? Look at how you've failed, yet again." Then shame whispers to us, "You are such an embarrassment. Lock that memory away. No one must ever know the real you." And then condemnation sinks its claws of despair into our hearts and pronounces its verdict: "*You* are the failure. *You* are the regret. *You belong to me.*"

Where do we turn when the regrets of our near or distant past haunt us like that?

While our nostalgia needs to be sent forward to the day of our glorification, our regrets need to be pushed further backward to the day of our justification. Backward, beyond the hypothetical "if only's" of mislived time. Backward, beyond the day of our birth. Backward, through the centuries, until those regrets collide with the cross.

At the cross, Jesus silenced the accusations of Satan. The apostle Paul asks in Romans 8:33, "Who shall bring any charge against God's elect?" daring any devil or man to answer. "It is God who justifies." His verdict cannot be overruled.

There at the cross, Jesus took the shame that walks hand in hand with our regrets. He severed it from us, once and for all, when he endured the shame of the cross (Hebrews 12:2). Shame loses its defining power when we remember that Jesus loved the *real* us, pouring the light of his mercy into the darkest parts of our story.

Our justification in history reminds us that "there is therefore now *no* condemnation for those who are in Christ Jesus" (Romans 8:1, my emphasis). "No" means *"not now, not ever"*. Your past becomes powerless to condemn when you learn to answer it with Paul, who asks, "Who is to condemn? Christ Jesus is the one who died—more than that, who was raised—who is at the right hand of God, who indeed is interceding for us" (v 34). We answer the memories that haunt us, and Satan's accusations against us, by remembering the truth about the God who loves us.

THE GOD WHO REMEMBERS... AND "FORGETS"

While our memory is important to our sense of identity, it is not ultimate. This is:

> *Your life is hidden with Christ in God. (Colossians 3:3)*

Standing before God one day, we will see that his faithful remembrance of us sustained us through every twist and turn of our lives. The God who knows us completely, "knows our frame; he remembers that we are dust" (Psalm 103:14). He does not search you for a heroic past but for honest trust in the present. And to those who trust their times into his hands—past, present and future—he says:

> *I will forgive their iniquity, and I will remember their sin no more. (Jeremiah 31:34)*
>
> *I, I am he who blots out your transgressions for my own sake, and I will not remember your sins. (Isaiah 43:25)*

According to these two Old Testament prophets, not only does God have perfect recall; he has perfect "forgetfulness". And in this way, my friend Ray Ortlund points out, even the accusations of Satan become vehicles through which the gospel may give us comfort.

> Satan, the accuser, comes before God and says, "Look at that Christian down there. Why do you still love him? Don't you remember what he did to you last week, and again on Tuesday, and then again yesterday?" And God says, if you'll allow me to put it this way, "No, I don't remember. Gabriel, where does that believer stand with us? Check the database." Gabriel logs on, but the only information that comes up on the screen is the righteousness of Christ freely credited to that sinner, because that's how God honors himself as God. "I blot out your transgressions, I splice your bad plays out of my game film, *for my own sake.*" So God says back to Satan, "I'm not saying your facts are wrong, but you're not telling the *whole* story about that Christian. What matters most to me, *for my own sake*, is not that person's record but Christ's record for him." That is grace. That is God. That is the way to revival.[32]

If your entire "life is hidden with Christ in God" (Colossians 3:3), then that includes your past. *Your past is hidden with*

Christ in God. Do you really believe that *that* is how God sees you?

When your time comes to an end, when your body is in the casket and your soul is before the Lord, when that which was once living in time is now a memory in the minds of those who remain here—God will remember and forget as only he can. Perfectly.

CHAPTER EIGHT

FUNERALS
Out of Time

"Death is a strange thing. People live their whole lives as if it does not exist, and yet it's often one of the great motivations for living. … We fear it, yet most of us fear more than anything that it may take someone other than ourselves. For the greatest fear of death is always that it will pass us by. And leave us there alone."

FREDRIK BACKMAN

None of us are really ready for our first brush with the reality of death. My youngest daughter certainly wasn't. Last year, through a deluge of tears, she said goodbye to one of her pets—an animal loved by a few yet loathed by most. It was a rat, named Sophie. And nobody had loved Sophie the way my daughter had loved Sophie. Cradling her dead rat, she sang between sobs a line from a song we'd sung countless times together as she was tucked in at night: "What can wash away my sins? Nothing but the blood of Jesus." The tears eventually subsided, and Sophie was reverently taken outside, where our daughter proceeded to push the lifeless rodent on a swing for the better part of an hour, sobbing quietly to herself, before she was able to be convinced that Sophie needed to be buried. And there the tears flowed again.

"The last enemy to be destroyed is death" (1 Corinthians 15:26). The goodbye of a funeral comes with a finality that is perhaps the most difficult emotion to navigate in this life. Yet, as my daughter will discover, the longer we live in this world, the more interactions with death we will have. And each one of those interactions acts as an alarm clock of sorts, alerting us to the unyielding fact that the time of every single creature in this world comes with an expiration date. Every life that begins ends. Every new entrance into humanity will have an exit. And so will we.

One of the recurring reminders in Scripture is that your life is a breath. And though we're all pretty good at denying it—like a sleeper hitting the snooze button again and again, refusing to leave the comfort of their dreamworld—eventually every one of us will wake up and face the truth of it.

Depending on where you live in the world, you will probably have around eight decades on this planet. At the time of writing, the average life expectancy tops out at around 85 years in places like Hong Kong and Japan. Where I live in Australia, it's approximately 83 years and it declines globally from here: Europe (79 years), USA (77 years), Latin America (75 years) and Africa (64 years). Like Jesus, who only walked this earth for 33 years, some of us will have much, much less time. Others might have a little more. But for the sake of a generous average, let's consider the nice round figure of 80 years.

If God gives you 80 years in the world, you will experience about 4,200 Sundays in your lifetime. If you're presently over the age of 40, you can halve that. If you're over the age of 60, that figure is probably somewhere in the hundreds. Only a few thousand times at most will we sit under the preaching of God's word and worship with our church. Only a few thousand times at most will we wake up and deal with those Monday morning blues. (God is merciful.)

James asks the question, "What is your life?" and then immediately answers: "You are a mist that appears for a little time and then vanishes" (James 4:14). The point that James is reminding us of is that regardless of how much time we are given, it still only amounts to "a little time". Consider how easily you might spend $4,200, if you were able to spend it on anything you desired. How quickly that money would go. It's the same with your weeks.

Your life is a mist.

A brief morning fog that lingers momentarily.

A vapour.

A breath.

BREATHS

Go ahead and take a deep breath in, hold it for a few seconds, and then breathe out.

In the space between that inhalation and exhalation—and likely a few more times while reading this sentence—your body, quite incredibly, transferred the oxygen of that breath to your blood cells (thus sustaining your life) and expelled the carbon dioxide that had been building up inside of you (also thus sustaining your life). This rhythmic back-and-forth is the miracle of life.

You are *alive*.

You are alive.

You did nothing to earn it, merit it or lay claim to it. This life was gifted to you, just as it was when God breathed into the first man and "the man became a living creature" (Genesis 2:7). The dates that will mark your tombstone will be the date of the first breath that your virgin lungs gasped upon entry into the world and the date of the final sigh that slowly exits your lips.

In fact, the idea of our "final breath" is a common way in which Scripture refers to death. When our breath expires, so too does our life. "Abraham *breathed his last* and died in a good old age, an old man and full of years, and was gathered to his people" (Genesis 25:8, my emphasis). "And Isaac *breathed his last*, and he died..." (35:29). And so on. Breathing indicates that we are alive.

But there is another indicator. Within moments of exiting the womb and entering the world, as our new lungs draw their first breath, we do something else for the first time: *cry*.

TEARS

Breaths and tears go together. Breathing and grieving belong to the living. As a pastor, I've shared tears with people in our church as we've sat in the room of 80-year olds, 30-year-olds, and one-day-olds whose breath had left their body. Only the living breathe—which means only the living cry. Funerals are an assembly of the breathing—consecrated with tears—in memory of the not-breathing.

Even Jesus wept at a funeral: a funeral that he knew full-well he was going to "wreck" with a resurrection. He turns up four days late at the graveside of his friend Lazarus and assures the dead man's sister Martha, "I am the resurrection and the life. Whoever believes in me, though he die, yet shall he live, and everyone who lives and believes in me shall never die" (John 11:25-26). Then he does something that surprises us. He weeps (v 35). The reason why this is surprising is that he *knows* that resurrection is coming. He *knows* that he and everyone there are minutes away from a spectacular reunion, when every sorrow will be turned into joy. Yet still he weeps. The one who rules over time is yet "a most tender and feeling Saviour".[33] Being faithfully present means that we enter into the lives of those around us, learning to "rejoice with those who rejoice, [and] weep with those who weep" (Romans 12:15).

But weeping with others brings home an unsettling truth. One day *our* time will end. We tend to not want to open that door. But here's what happens when we're brave enough to be honest about our creaturely mortality: we gain perspective. There are two important truths we need to press into our hearts if we are to live faithfully present in the days God gives us. First, we must learn to number our days, for our final day will come sooner than we think. Second, we must remember that in Christ, our final day is not our final day.

LEARNING TO NUMBER YOUR DAYS

Death has a way of putting our experience of time into a clearer light. Most of us, most of the time, are not thinking about death. And certainly not about our death—which is why, if we are forced to wait a *whole hour* in traffic or *a whole ten minutes* at the drive-through, we'll grumble to a friend, "It took *forever.*" But the moment we honestly consider that there is a day on the calendar that will indeed be *our* last day, suddenly 80 years of life—4,200 Sundays—feels very, very short.

You know your birthday. But none of us know our death-day. Yet one day, on an appointed date known by God alone (Job 14:5), you will breathe *your* final breath. One day, your time in this world will be memorialised with a name etched on a gravestone or an urn that holds your ashes. And a hundred years from your final day, when the world has all new people, you will be to that time somebody who lived *a long time ago.*

The Scriptures that teach us that God has numbered our days (e.g. Psalm 139:16) exhort us to do likewise. In Psalm 39, David helps us consider the brevity of our lives, praying, "LORD, make me aware of my end and the number of my days so that I will know how short-lived I am. In fact, you have made my days just inches long, and my life span is as nothing to you. Yes, every human being stands as only a vapour. *Selah*" (v 4-5, CSB).

In Psalm 90, Moses uses similar language and compares our temporariness with the timelessness of God. He begins by remembering God's timelessness—that "before you gave birth to the earth and the world, from eternity to eternity, you are God" (v 2, CSB). To the God who created the concept of time, "a thousand years are like yesterday that passes by, like a few hours of the night" (v 4, CSB). In contrast, humanity is like grass that appears in the morning, has its day in the sun and is withered by evening (v 5-6). Then Moses prays in verse 12, "So teach us to number our days that we may get a heart of wisdom". In other words, foolishness is living in such a way that we never consider our end. Wisdom is gained by remembering that our lives are brief and that our every breath is a gift from God (Job 12:10). The one who has numbered with absolute precision the number of stars in the universe and knows them each by name (Psalm 147:4) has numbered your breaths and the days of your life. How precious each of them is.

One of the accounts I follow on Twitter is called "Daily Death Reminder". Each day this account sends out the same unchanging message: "You will die someday". And even though I know what it's going to say, every time I read it, my breath catches a little. Some days, the reminder makes me smile. On others, it causes me to reconsider everything in my life. But the truth is, I need to be reminded because, probably like you, I have a tendency to fill my days with so many things: a mixture of both deeply meaningful things and completely meaningless things—all of which frequently distract me from considering the shortness of my life.

Let me ask you a few questions to help press the importance of this down deep.

Were God to reveal to you that this year would be your final year in the world, what would look different about your life? How would the way you speak to those around you change? Which friends and loved ones would you pursue with greater intentionality? Who would you reach out to and try to make peace with? What trivial and worthless activities that presently devour your precious time would you immediately put away? How would the intensity of your expressed love change toward each person in front of you?

There is liberation in being honest about our end. I've been in a handful of very dangerous situations in my time in this world, where I walked away thankful to still be breathing. Each of them put the brevity of my life into focus. Each of them made me want to love my family and friends and church with greater intensity. Each of them made me treasure the days I've been given. If none of us are promised tomorrow (James 4:13-14), how inexpressibly valuable is every day that we wake into and bless with the name "*today*". The most seemingly ordinary days of our lives are, each and every one, an undeserved grace.

Yet we also need to remember that when our days conclude, and the final credits roll, and death puts us in the ground, this will not be the end for those who belong to Jesus. In Christ, death is not the end of life but the doorway into fullness of life.

THE BURNING HATRED OF THE LOVE OF CHRIST

Deep down, we all have a sense that death—the most natural fate in the world for all living creatures—is unnatural. And it is; it's an unwelcome intruder that broke into this world through our first parents' sin in Genesis 3. The presence of death is the hellish consequence of the original and ultimate sin: walking away from the Author of life. And yet still we feel it: death doesn't belong here. "Death is the Great Interruption," writes Tim Keller, "tearing loved ones away from us, or us from them ... Death is our Great Enemy, more than anything. It makes a claim on each and every one of us, pursuing us relentlessly through all our days."[34]

And Jesus burns with holy hatred toward it.

You see, back at the graveside of Lazarus, Jesus did more than just shed a few tears. John tells us that he was "deeply moved in his spirit and greatly troubled" (John 11:33). This was more than just compassion or being touched with pity. This was a sanctified fury. Your Bible probably has a footnote on the phrase "deeply moved" (ESV: "indignant"; CSB: "angry") to better capture the emotion of Jesus in this scene. The actual verb, used literally, translates as "to snort like an angry horse; to roar with rage".

The Lord Jesus, standing at the grave of Lazarus, is growling at death. In a sense, he is looking at the great enemy of humanity square in the eye and through the rage-stained tears of divine love, saying, "Death, I'm coming for you". The 19th-century Princeton theologian B.B. Warfield writes:

> The spectacle of the distress of Mary and her companions enraged Jesus ... Inextinguishable fury seizes upon him ... It is death that is the object of his wrath, and behind death him who has the power of death, and whom he has come into the world to destroy. Tears of sympathy may fill his eyes, but ... his soul is held by rage: and he advances to the tomb, in Calvin's words, "as a champion who prepares for conflict".[35]

Moments later, the one who is "the resurrection and the life", would reveal the glory of his power. The voice that had called the universe into being would command the very dead Lazarus out of the grave and back to life. And within a few of weeks of this day, Jesus would face death himself. That was why he came; he was born to die—to reverse the curse of sin and inflict the mortal wound that will put death to death. And he would accomplish this by going down into death itself, absorbing the full weight of the curse of our sin upon himself, and crushing it with his resurrection. It's why, in his magnificent chapter on the resurrection, 1 Corinthians 15, the apostle Paul mocks our great enemy: "O death, where is your victory? O death, where is your sting?" (v 55). What gives him the confidence to mock the mighty leveller of humanity? In Christ, death is conquered.

DEATH WON'T HAVE THE FINAL WORD

In the here and now, we will indeed still grieve over the presence of death as it crosses our path. For as long as sin exists, so too will death, "for the wages of sin is death" (Romans 6:23). But we need no longer fear it. For even our final enemy, under the sovereignty of Jesus, will be forced to serve us. Death may indeed be the final enemy (1 Corinthians 15:26); but for the believer, death is now just a butler who opens the door and ushers us into fullness of joy in the presence of God (Psalm 16:11).

In Christ, our future is *resurrection*: life everlasting, unpunctuated by sadness and free from final goodbyes. It is a future that neither time nor the devil nor death have the power to ever take away from us. And that's why Christians across the centuries have faced death with a smile on their faces and a song on their lips.

Like Lady Jane Grey—the 17-year-old cousin of the infamously ruthless queen of England known today as "Bloody Mary". Jane had discovered the doctrines of grace preached by Martin Luther and was subsequently condemned to death for treason in 1554. Before she was executed, however, Jane wrote a note to her younger sister on the inside of her Bible that read, "This is the book .... which shall lead you to the path of eternal joy ... And as touching my death, rejoice as I do, good sister, that I shall be delivered of this corruption, and put on incorruption. For I am assured that I shall for losing a mortal life, win an immortal life."[36]

Or like Tim, a young man whose family attended my church, who was diagnosed with incurable bowel cancer just a few years ago at the age of 30. Yet through his cancer, Tim came to trust in the saving love of Jesus. As his condition got worse, he spent his final months sharing his hope in Christ with the doctors, nurses and friends who came into his room. When told by a well-meaning but misguided friend, "God is going to heal you, Tim; you just have to believe it", Tim responded, "I believe he can. And I'm praying that he does a miracle like that. But even if he doesn't, I'm ok. Because then soon, I'll get to be with him." Tim died young, yet he died well.

Or like the apostle Paul, probably in his early sixties, writing some of his final words from a Roman prison before he was executed for the sake of Christ. From here, the former persecutor of the church declared, "The time for my departure is close. I have fought the good fight, I have finished the race, I have kept the faith. There is reserved for me the crown of righteousness, which the Lord, the righteous Judge, will give me on that day, and not only to me, but to all those who have loved his appearing" (2 Timothy 4:6-8 CSB).

Our time here will end. But the brevity of our time in this world need not be a cause for fear when we see our lives through the lens of the resurrection and learn to say with Paul, "For me to live is Christ, and to die is gain" (Philippians 1:21). That is how Christians die well: we remember that while our days are numbered, our lives are eternal. While our breaths will eventually come to an end, the faithful love of Christ our Saviour will not. So when the day comes when our number is called, and we feel the fingers of death reaching out to take hold of our hand, we need not be afraid where it will lead us. Under the lordship of Jesus, death can only bless us. As one Puritan put it, death for the Christian is little more than "the funeral of all our sorrows".[37]

Part 2:
Place

CHAPTER NINE

HERE
Earthly Places

"There can be no such thing as a 'global village.' No matter how much one may love the world as a whole, one can live fully in it only by living responsibly in some small part of it."
WENDELL BERRY

Having attended seven different schools across my twelve years of grade school, it's little wonder that a sense of rootedness to a physical place isn't something I grew up with. The first time I moved between countries, at the age of eleven, my family left the small beachside holiday town of Noosa in Australia to help plant a church across the world in a place where rolling plains met soaring snowy mountains: Denver, USA.

Up until that point, life in Noosa had been all I really knew. I had everything that a sports-obsessed, eleven-year-old Australian kid could dream of—friends, teams, opportunities and good weather—and I had to leave it all behind to move to the Mile High City, which barely even had oxygen, let alone a single friend in the kinds of schools I'd only seen in the movies. During that decade of life and the next one, I would move internationally a total of six times: a little over once every three years before I reached the age of 30. But, as is usually the case, that first one hit the hardest.

To move from Noosa to Denver was to experience a number of jarring changes. We exchanged a small town for a big city; the beach for the mountains; a mainly outdoor life for a mainly indoor life. While our family had never had lots of money, back in Australia we never seemed to lack for anything. But the international move hit our family in the wallet. Hard. Our first couple of years in Denver were spent living in other people's basements and eating the free meals in the school cafeteria reserved for kids from low-income families. It didn't take me long to figure out how to hustle these wealthy American kids for a better-quality lunch by offering to stand in the long cafeteria lines and bring them their food for a few extra bucks. Most days, this immigrant from Australia ate well, thanks to my 1990s version of middle-school Uber Eats.

But the truth was that I didn't want to be *here,* where I was. I wanted to be back *there*, where I had come from. I was desperately homesick for the sense of belonging and familiarity I had known in my former place.

Slowly our roots began to go down into our new soil and find anchor points. Soon I realised that not everything about my new place was bad. In fact, the first noticeable difference that was particularly wonderful was our first white Christmas. Sweaty Christmas Days spent playing cricket and lawn bowls in the backyard were now spent throwing snowballs, going sledding, and then coming inside to warm up by the fireplace. No longer were we "dreaming of a white Christmas"; we were living it!

Before long, those roots found stability. Close friends were made. I started dating a girl in high school named Kristina (who I continue to date 23 years later, now as my wife), and my heart began to settle and treasure our new place as home. So when my family decided to move back to Australia for my last two years of high school, I didn't want to be back *there*. Home had become *here*, where I was, and I didn't want to leave.

Perhaps that's one of the tensions of leaving a place; part of our heart gets left behind. And there's a temptation to spend the rest of our lives longing to be in more than one place at once because we misguidedly think that by doing that we'll be whole again. But the God over all time is the God of all places. Omnipresence belongs to him alone. We can only faithfully exist in one place at one time. To be human means making peace with that.

While time limits us by way of duration, place limits us by way of location. No matter who or where you are in the world right now, God has given you three aspects of place that locate you. The first is your geography. The second is your body. The third is your relationships. Then, to those who are in Christ, he gives a fourth feature that acts as the true north on our compass, guiding the other three aspects: a heavenly citizenship—a future place which shapes life in the present. Over the remaining chapters of this book, we're going to explore each of these God-ordained limitations of place and the ways in which he calls us to practise faithful presence within them.

Let's again begin where the Bible itself begins: "In the beginning, God created the heavens and the earth" (Genesis 1:1).

THE LIMITATION OF PLACE

Genesis 1 – 2 is a story of place. God creates a universe and fills it with his creative beauty, declaring goodness over every part of it. In Genesis 1, place is universal: the entire created cosmos is in view. In that sense, place is something we can never escape. "Place," says one philosopher, "is as requisite as the air we breathe, the ground on which we stand, the bodies we have. We are surrounded by places. We walk over them and through them. We live in places, relate to others in them, die in them. Nothing we do is unplaced."[38] Our entire existence plays out within the confines of matter, time and place; and God created all of it. Whether it's heaven, earth, or anywhere else—wherever we can point to and say "there", that "there" has been created by and is inhabited by an omnipresent God.

But something important happens in Genesis 2, as humanity comes into focus. Here, place is localised. Humanity inhabits a specific place—Eden, within the planet we call Earth—and is entrusted with its stewardship.

> [7]*Then the* LORD *God formed the man out of the dust from the ground and breathed the breath of life into his nostrils, and the man became a living being.* [8]*The* LORD *God planted a garden in Eden, in the east, and there he placed the man he had formed ...* [15]*The* LORD *God took the man and placed him in the garden of Eden to work it and watch over it.* (Genesis 2:7-8, 15, CSB)

The first gift that God gave to the first human being was *life with him* (v 7). The second gift was *a place to belong to and watch over* (v 8, 15). Man was embodied with life and then embedded into a location. A few verses later, God gave his third gift: *human relationships marked by love* (v 18-25). This was the world which God created and called good: a world hedged by limits.

And while we are often tempted to believe that fullness of life would be found in casting off our limits—in escaping from what we deem as "ordinary life" in order to be somewhere more important or satisfying, in being anywhere other than where we are right now—the early chapters of Genesis tell a different story. The glory of Eden was simply life with God, in a particular place, loving others. And it was perfect.

Here we see what it is to be faithfully present to God and others, in the place God has put us in—here we see what it is that really matters. As the author Zack Eswine puts it:

> To daily orient your life toward a moment-by-moment relationship with God … attending to God's work among the faces, names, and stories where you are is to do already what God considers significant … to dwell knowledgeably and hospitably in the place God gives you is to glorify him.[39]

As Adam and Eve were called to the practice of faithful presence within the garden, so too are we within the various places God has put us in.

Just as we live in a "now", we also live in a "here". And wherever *here* is, it is the exact geographic location that God calls you to treat with attentiveness and care.

So think about the place you are presently in: what the people are like; how the land is shaped; the collective identity of those who live near you and the things they hold dear. I don't know how long you've been there or how long you're intending on staying. But for as long as you dwell there, God desires that your presence would bless *that* place. Where you are deeply matters to God.

THE FIRST QUESTION GOD EVER ASKED

In fact, did you know that the very first question God asked in the Bible was a question regarding *place*? After Adam and Eve disobeyed God—by grasping to be what only he is, by throwing off the limits he had built into their humanity—they hid themselves. So God asked Adam, "Where are you?" (Genesis 3:9). This is not the kind of question that an omniscient, omnipresent, universe-creating God asks for his own sake, as if he had lost track of Adam, like a distracted parent in a crowded shopping centre. He asked the question for Adam's sake.

Where are you?

The question "Where are you?" spoke not only to Adam's geographic location but also his relational location, with regards to God, others and himself. It demanded that he consider not only his present status but the status of his presence.

No longer was Adam walking with God but hiding from God.

No longer was he faithfully present but fearfully withdrawn.

No longer was he "naked and unashamed", but now he cowered in the shadows, clothed with guilt.

On that fateful day, the relationship between humanity and God, humanity itself, and humanity and the created world itself, was cursed. And one key consequence of humanity's rebellion was their removal from the garden. They were *displaced*. The South African theologian Craig Bartholomew points out, "Human identity is deeply bound up with place, and in Genesis 3 *displacement* is at the heart of God's judgment".[40]

From that day to this day, to the day Christ returns just as he promised, we will experience the effects of displacement. We'll frequently feel dislocated, ill at ease or not at home. Wherever we are in this world, we will find ourselves confronted with futility and pain and troubles and brokenness. We will face circumstances in every place we live in that make us shake our head while longing for renewal.

And still, along the way, just like our first parents, we too will be tempted to cast off our humanity, grasp for divinity and attempt to put ourselves in the place of God. Perhaps in no greater way do we experience this temptation today—the desire to transcend where we presently are—than through the small rectangular screens that we carry around in our pockets.

OUR DISEMBODIED DIGITAL AGE

While wandering daydreamers and distracted deep-thinkers have existed in every time and place, inhabiting a mental world of one's own was previously always a solo and internalised experience. Yet those of us alive in the 21st century find ourselves inhabiting the early stages of a new epoch in human history: the Digital Age.

I'm old enough to remember educational life before the internet, when one had to borrow books from the library and use a hardback set of encyclopaedias in order to write a school assignment. The internet connected us to information in new ways. But it also connected us to each other in new ways. Social networks gave people a platform from which to interact globally and instantly with one another. It allowed us to reconnect with those from places we'd formerly lived in and gave us a window into one another's daily lives.

But online platforms have also provided us with the ability to disconnect from where we are and those around us, in order to be digitally present somewhere else. Social networks and video technology have given us an illusion of something that belongs to God alone: omnipresence. We can see what's happening in other parts of the world in real time. We can cast our presence to multiple places simultaneously and interact with those there. Like a drug, our digital mobility provides a high of being able to escape from where we are, whenever we want to. But, like a drug, it's addictive, and the addiction is enslaving.

Ride any bus, train or subway and try to find more than a person or two whose head is not bowed to their screen, as they escape from their present *here* to some distant *there*. Let's be honest: we've reached a point in Western society such that were we to see someone at our local coffee shop merely looking around, with no headphones in their ears, making eye contact with others and smiling, most of us would suspect that we might be in the presence of a serial killer. Ours is a time of social disembeddedness; much more often than not, we seek connection through the portal in our pockets rather than with the people where we are.

And our malady goes far deeper than just our social behaviour when out in public. Even in the places where we're with those we love most—the places we call "*home*"—how frequently is time together that of "absent others",[41] who are physically located in the same room, yet digitally connected elsewhere? American comedian Bo Burnham, who rose to fame through YouTube, spoke for many in our times when he said only half-jokingly, "The non-digital world is merely a theatrical space in which one stages and records content for the much more real, much more vital digital space".[42]

Yet, despite the powerful gravity of the online world, we know that Burnham's quip isn't true. The real world remains fundamental. When my wife walked into my study today, carrying a genuine grief over the suicide of Stephen "tWitch" Boss, one of her favourite performers on social media, it wasn't because she could no longer watch him dance. Her sadness came from the irreversible fact that tWitch—a DJ and dancer known for his big smile and fun synchronised dances with his wife and three children—was no longer *here*. We may come and go from the digital world as we please. But when we exit the non-digital world—the world where we *actually* are—our departure is permanent.

The Digital Age has simultaneously given birth to unprecedented levels of connectivity and loneliness. We are in touch with one another but not really known. As it turns out, an escapist life disembodied from the limits of God-given place is not the way back to Eden at all. It's how we broke the world in the first place.

What if we were to reject unlimitedness as the soul-crushing reality that it is (for any mere mortal, at least), and instead give ourselves with renewed energy to where God has us? I'm not necessarily advocating a full-scale digital withdrawal (though perhaps, for some, an extended social-media sabbatical is long overdue). There is much good in our ability to connect instantaneously with others around the world that I am grateful for. What I am advocating, however—what *must* be prioritised by followers of the incarnated one as non-negotiable for healthy discipleship in this world—is *attentiveness* to the place we are in.

Let's commit to being present *here*, for as long as we are here. To spending "less time watching others live their lives … and more time living our own".[43] To relearning what it means to be in the place where our feet are.

LEARNING TO BE WHERE YOUR FEET ARE

Perhaps what we need is a smaller view of the world. While I love being able to get on a plane and be in another part of the planet within a day or so—and while I am thankful for the way that social networks have introduced me to all kinds of wonderful people that I probably would have never connected with otherwise—the truth is that I can only dwell in, work in and watch over one place at a time. To be faithfully present means that I cannot love the world generally or theoretically; I must love it particularly. To repeat the words of Wendell Berry that we began this chapter with, "No matter how much one may love the world as a whole, one can live fully in it only by living responsibly in some small part of it".[44]

Have you ever considered that the perfect world of Eden was a roadless world? Roads are built for getting us somewhere. And while there was certainly a sense of expansion in God's command to "fill the earth and subdue it" (Genesis 1:28), the good life was not found in getting somewhere but in dwelling somewhere.

The predominant cultural metaphor for success in our time is that of the road. "They're going to go far in life," we say of a young high achiever. The road is where we "find ourselves" and discover what matters in life, as evidenced by the plot line of almost every single friends-on-a-roadtrip film.

The adventure and unknowns of a transient life, a life on the road, are undoubtedly alluring. We live in an age of widespread wanderlust. But Eswine gives a reality check to those of us who find we are always going, always moving, always imagining what it would be like to be somewhere else: "Eventually, you get to where you're going. Have you thought of that? It's one thing to do what you need to in order to get somewhere. It's quite another to know how to stay put for a while once you've gotten there."[45]

To be sure, some of us may have vocations that require the kind of mobility exhibited by the apostle Paul, who would spend a couple of years in a place planting a church and proclaiming Jesus and then move on to the next place to do more of the same. These days, many of us are likely to have experienced a significant move or relocation at some point in our lives. It's also true that the gospel will not advance into places where it currently is not unless some of us take it there.

But even when Paul was only in a place temporarily, he loved deeply. His letters reveal his desire to be present with those he had left behind. Hear how his heart bleeds through his words! To Timothy he says, "As I remember your tears, I long to see you, that I may be filled with joy" (2 Timothy 1:4). To the church he planted in Philippi he writes, "For God is my witness, how I yearn for you all with the affection of Christ Jesus" (Philippians 1:8). He tells those in Thessalonica with whom he lived for only a matter of months that "after we were forced to leave you for a short time (in person, not in heart), we greatly desired and made every effort to return and see you face to face" (1 Thessalonians 2:17, CSB).

Wherever Paul was, he was all there. And so it must be with us. Wherever we live, we must be willing to give our heart and attentiveness to that place. To learn to confess with Jacob, "Surely the LORD is in *this* place, and I did not know it" (Genesis 28:16, my emphasis). We can be thankful for the technology that creates the sense of a global village. But let's commit to being known in the local one. The attention economy driven by clicks and likes in the digital world will repeatedly try to trick us into believing that real life is attained by being where we're *not*—that to be fully present where we are is to somehow be missing out on what's happening with everyone else, everywhere else.

The transient formative years of my teens and twenties taught me to become adaptable. But more and more, I am learning to remain: to put down roots and be faithfully present to a particular people in a particular place. My hope is that that's something you'll learn too.

Because the God who fills all places is right here in your present place.

Here, among all the beautiful ordinariness of where you presently are.

Here, among these people, in this place.

Here, where your feet are.

That is where God wants you to fully be.

CHAPTER TEN

BODIES
Human Places

*"Christianity is almost the only one of the great religions
which thoroughly approves of the body—which believes that
matter is good, that God Himself once took on a human
body, that some kind of body is going to be given to us even in
Heaven and is going to be an essential part of our happiness,
our beauty and our energy."*

C.S. LEWIS

One relationship we don't often consider is our relationship
to our bodies. Like the gravity that pins us to the
ground or the abundance of oxygen that is right now keeping
us alive, our bodies are an often-overlooked part of reality
that is fundamental to our existence. To be a human is to be
embodied.

Your body is incredible. I'm not complimenting your
appearance (though I'm sure you look great); I'm admiring
your existence.

Consider the intricacy of the human eyes: a pair of small,
delicate spheres, shielded by little more than a thin layer of
skin, that are able to detect around a million colour-variations
and are right now sending videographic evidence of every
event happening around you, along with every piece of
information in front of you (including this very description),

to your brain, which receives, comprehends, interacts with and can even store those files as memories for later use.

Then consider your brain: the command centre of your body, which instantly processes not only the video testimony of the eyes but the sounds received by the ears—converting the noises made by other human mouths into a shared, intelligible communication that is the basis of every relationship you have. Your brain is also receiving the smells taken in by the nose, the tastes detected by the tongue, and the sensation of touch being received by innumerable nerve endings in your body that provide the experiences of both pleasure and pain. And your brain does all of this simultaneously while coordinating the movements of your skeletal structure, making decisions, recalling memories and learning new information on the fly. Surely, as the psalmist declared, you are "fearfully and wonderfully made" (Psalm 139:14)!

Yet at the same time, our human bodies are fragile.

In fact, it doesn't take much for any one of the various parts of our body to break, or for our body as a whole to break down. If these bodies of ours don't receive constant care, sustenance, water, oxygen and rest, they stop working and, eventually, stop living. Add a single toxic ingredient into the system that isn't meant to be there—like cyanide or a deadly germ—and life will leave us within minutes. And we haven't even mentioned how every human body that *is* living is also somewhere on the well-trodden path of dying.

Numerous studies have shown that the growth we experience through our childhood and teen years hits a peak somewhere around the age of 25. From there, our bodies begin to physiologically decline. There's a reason why most professional athletes in any kind of high-impact sport (except those named Tom Brady) typically retire well before they reach 40 years of age: their bodies can't continue performing at the high level their sport requires of them.

While most of us aren't professional athletes, if we're past a certain age, we've probably noticed the same decline. In my teens and twenties, I regularly played rugby, basketball and a handful of other sports. My body took countless hits without serious injury. Muscle pain and soreness were normal but subsided quickly. Then, somewhere in my early thirties, a whole new epoch of human existence opened up to me: I discovered the thrilling possibility of experiencing significant and unexpected injury from all kinds of *other* activities, such as getting out of a chair, waking up in the morning or turning to look at something on my left.

As incredible as the human body is in complexity and design, its fragility reminds us that we are yet creaturely and dependent. It is this tension that marks our present existence. A vital part of living faithfully present to the life we have is learning to make peace with the body we've received. Flourishing in our own skin means refusing to treat our body as unimportant or as all-important, but as part of who we are, which is profoundly important to God. And that means our bodies, like the rest of life, need to be seen through the lens of the gospel.

CREATION: OUR "VERY GOOD" BODIES

In the beginning, God created the heavens and the earth by simply declaring that they *be*. And so they *were*. Genesis 1 tells us that after each component of the universe was spoken into being *ex nihilo*—"out of nothing"—God looked at each part and saw that it was good.

But when it came to creating us, he didn't speak us. He sculpted us: man out of the dust and woman out of man. The omnipotent Orator became a scrupulous artist, bending down and getting his hands dirty in the work of creating human bodies.

> *Then the* LORD *God formed the man of dust from the ground and breathed into his nostrils the breath of life, and the man became a living creature. (Genesis 2:7)*

> *Then the* LORD *God said, "It is not good that the man should be alone; I will make him a helper fit for him" ... So the* LORD *God caused a deep sleep to fall upon the man, and while he slept took one of his ribs and closed up its place with flesh. And the rib that the* LORD *God had taken from the man he made into a woman and brought her to the man. (v 18, 21-22)*

Humanity was God's creative grand finale. And only then did he declare that what he had made was "very good" (1:31). Think about that: everything God had made up to this point—the unique glory of each galaxy; the countless stars, whose names and number are known only by him; the beauty of this world in its original state of pre-curse purity; the creative diversity of every living creature in the sky, on land and in the sea—all of it was a warm-up for the creation of the first two human bodies.

That we are made from the dust of the ground should humble us. That our bodies are made by the hands of God himself should cause us to give thanks for them and treat them with the dignity they deserve. An embodied existence is a divine idea.

FALL: OUR GROANING, DYING BODIES

When Adam and Eve rebelled against God, the "very good" human bodies that God had created became corrupted and cursed. Humanity was separated from God—exiled from his presence. And the effects were immediate and devastating. Imagine a beautiful family portrait that is washed out from exposure to the sun. So became our first parents when they exposed the created world—which God had entrusted to their keeping—to sin. As a portrait once vibrant and alive with colourful detail becomes cracked and warped and discoloured, so went humanity. It's still true that we have been made by God and bear his image, and therefore retain great value and dignity—but the original glory has faded. Before, human bodies were fully and gloriously alive; now, we inhabit what Paul describes as a "body of death" (Romans 7:24). Before, human eyes could behold the glory of God, meeting him face to face, walking with him in the garden; now, none can see him and live (Exodus 33:20). Through the sin of humanity the entire world was broken and, to this day, groans under the weight of the curse as it awaits its promised redemption (Romans 8:20-22).

But while the fracture from the fall is universal, its greatest point of impact is felt in the place where the cosmic crime was committed: the human body. Australian scholar John Kleinig points out the flow of consequences in Genesis 3 that are all experienced within our bodies:

> It is the body that suffers the most obvious penalty …
> The woman experiences trouble in childbearing and
> pain in childbirth … The man has to work hard to
> make a living, because the ground no longer cooperates
> productively with him (3:17–19). But worst of all, God
> himself banishes them from the garden and shuts the
> gate to the tree of life. They live in exile apart from
> intimate, life-giving contact with him (3:23–24). By its
> banishment from God's presence, the body is diminished
> and doomed to die.[46]

REDEMPTION: GOD BECAME EMBODIED

Even more astounding than the Genesis 1 truth that God created our bodies is the John 1 truth that he was willing to humble himself in a body, permanently adding humanity to his deity. In Jesus, God the Son *became embodied*. To "incarnate" is to "become enfleshed" or to "put on flesh". The incarnation of Christ, remembered each Christmas by millions of Christians around the world, is the miracle of all miracles: Jesus, the Word of God, who bore the universe into existence, was born into the world. God Eternal entered into time. God Almighty, unlimited in strength and energy, took on flesh and the limitations of a human body.

> *In the beginning was the Word, and the Word was with God, and the Word was God. He was in the beginning with God. All things were made through him, and without him was not any thing made that was made ... And the Word became flesh and dwelt among us. (John 1:1-3, 14)*

Capturing the magnitude of this moment, the early Church Father Augustine wrote, "He was created of a mother whom He created. He was carried by hands that He had formed."[47] That God is the Creator of our bodies shows that embodied humanity matters to him. But that God himself *took on a body* in the incarnation, going on to be bodily crucified and bodily resurrected, reveals *just how much* our embodied selves matter to him. Through the actions in the body of the first Adam, all were corrupted by sin. But through the actions in the body of Jesus Christ—the second Adam—all who believe will be made whole (Romans 1:16; 5:19).

In his book *What God Has to Say about Our Bodies*, one of the best books written to-date on this subject, Sam Allberry helps us see just how pro-body God really is:

> Jesus's incarnation is the highest compliment the human body has ever been paid. God not only thought our bodies up and enjoyed putting several billion of them together; he made one for himself. And not just for the Christmas season ... No. His body was for life. And for

far more than that. After his death he was raised bodily. And after his resurrection he returned to his Father in heaven, also bodily ... There is now a human body sitting at the right hand of God the Father at the very center of heaven. Bodies matter ... He became what he valued enough to redeem.[48]

This runs contrary to the heresy known as Gnosticism—a false teaching that has repeatedly sprung up over the centuries, which rejects the bodily life of Christ, scorns physical matter as inherently evil, and seeks to escape an embodied life for a higher plane of spirituality. The incarnation of Jesus in this world reveals that our salvation goes much further than simply "saving our soul"—the immaterial part of what makes up our "self". Jesus came to redeem every part of us; that includes "the redemption of our bodies" (Romans 8:23). Your eternal future in Christ will not be that of a disembodied spirit but that of your spirit in your resurrected and glorified body.

RENEWAL: YOUR ETERNAL FUTURE IN CHRIST IS AN EMBODIED ONE

What Jesus experienced in the body, he promises to share with his people. As Paul writes, "If we have been united with him in a death like his, we shall certainly be united with him in a resurrection like his" (Romans 6:5). Have you ever considered that the eternal life Christ has promised you is one in a resurrected body like his? Heaven is going to be glorious beyond our wildest imagination, but our home in heaven as it is right now, on this side of Christ's return, will be temporary. Heaven will be a wonderful layover on our way to our final destination of a renewed world in the new creation (Revelation 21:1-3). And there, in the new creation, "the Lord Jesus Christ ... will transform our lowly body to be like his glorious body" (Philippians 3:20-21). Our bodies will be raised from the grave and infused with a glory akin to the glory of the resurrected body of Jesus.

In this way, the bodily resurrection of Jesus is not a one-off cosmic anomaly; it's a precedent. It is our definite future, guaranteed in our present through the down payment of the Holy Spirit indwelling the heart of every believer (Ephesians 1:13-14; 2 Corinthians 1:22; 5:1-5). In eternity you will still be you but magnificently so.

What does all this mean? It means that your body shouldn't be worshipped as an ultimate thing, nor should it be treated as a common thing. As far as God is concerned, your earthly body, made of physical matter, matters. And one day, it will be renewed in Christ's likeness. So while we should care for our bodies and steward them well in the way we eat, exercise and rest, we should also not be afraid when they start to wear out. In fact, we can face our inevitable bodily decline with a holy smirk. Every new crease that appears on our face, along with every new grey hair that appears on our head, is nothing more than a reminder that we are a little bit closer to the day when Jesus "will transform our lowly body to be like his glorious body" (Philippians 3:21). When we get sick or find ourselves battling chronic pain, we still bring it to the Lord in prayer, asking for healing and relief as Scripture instructs us to do (James 5:14-15). But our ultimate hope is not in a temporary restoration of our health; it is in the promise of him "who was seated on the throne [who] said, 'Behold, I am making all things new'" (Revelation 21:5).

The point I want you to see is that that body of yours is loved by God. It is a good gift from him, blemished and broken by sin to be sure but in Christ redeemed and on its way to being gloriously resurrected. According to Jesus, rightly loving God and trusting God includes not only your whole heart, mind and soul... but also "all your strength" (Mark 12:30): that is, your physical body. And the fact that

God requires "all" our strength illustrates that our bodies are limited not only with regards to what they can do and where they can be but in whom they ultimately belong to.

BELONGING: THE LIMITATION OF INTIMACY

When we look at our bodies through the lens of the gospel, the big idea we come away with is this: our bodies matter, but they are not our own. We are indeed called to be good stewards of our bodies, but stewardship does not mean sovereignty. In 1 Corinthians 6, Paul was writing to a group of believers who had fallen for the lie that what they did with their bodies was of little or no consequence. Apparently, some within the church at Corinth had misunderstood grace as a license to do whatever they felt like. Sayings like "All things are lawful for me" (v 12) had snuck into their collective vocabulary—which sounds eerily similar to some of the slogans popular in our own time of expressive individualism that diminish bodily responsibility, like "If it feels good, do it", "My body, my choice" and "Follow your heart".

The result for the Corinthians was a low view of their bodies and a casual view of sex. Paul therefore reminds them, "The body is not meant for sexual immorality, but for the Lord, and the Lord for the body" (v 13). He warns them to take the sacredness of their bodies seriously and to "flee from sexual immorality" (v 18). "Or do you not know," he goes on to say, "that your body is a temple of the Holy Spirit within you, whom you have from God? You are not your own, for you were bought with a price. So glorify God in your body" (v 19-20).

Here's the bottom line: your body does not primarily belong to you. It belongs to God. And true intimacy, of the covenantal kind, always requires exclusivity. In the same way that a husband and wife *belong* to one another—and to physically betray the exclusivity of that belonging is adultery—so it is spiritually. To belong to God is to embrace the sacred limit and exclusivity of that relationship. As author Alan Noble points out, "Belonging necessitates limits. The question is to whom we belong. If we belong to ourselves, then we set our own limits—which means we have no limits except our own will. If we belong to God, then knowing and abiding by His limits enables us to live as we were created to live, as the humans He designed us to be."[49] God has limited how we use our bodies because the intimacy of our belonging to him—of our bodies being "members of Christ" (v 15)—matters more than we could imagine.

The story of Genesis 1 – 3 provides the necessary framework for you to think rightly about the body—about *your* body, with all its history, with all its flaws and imperfections, with all its visible and invisible scars that bear witness to the sharp edges of an embodied life in this world. It is true that every human body born into the world this side of Genesis 3 will be marred by the fall and experience the effects of pain, disease, illness, injury, physical decline and eventually death. But it is also true that every human body—that *your* human body—is highly esteemed by God.

In this way, every human body is a living, breathing bundle of paradoxes. Bodies are beautifully made yet broken by sin; eternally valuable yet deteriorating in real time; extraordinarily designed yet frustratingly ordinary; a gift we have received yet a responsibility we will give an account for; integral to our sense of self yet not the sum of our self; a flimsy dwelling like a tent (2 Corinthians 5:2-4) yet a temple for the Holy Spirit (1 Corinthians 6:19-20). For God so loved this world of precious, broken-bodied people that he came to save us by becoming embodied himself.

At the risk of overstating the obvious, being faithfully present requires faithfulness in the way we live life in the body. Your body is the sacred place in which faithful presence to God, and to every single person you encounter this week, is enacted. That body of yours, through which you walk and talk and live and love and eat and drink and laugh and grieve, is the body that Jesus promises to glorify. Because it has a future, how you treat it in the present is of great importance. Because we are not our own, our highest bodily aim is to glorify God with our bodies (v 20). Because our bodies are both important and eternal, we are to embrace the limitations that God has set upon them for our flourishing and go all-in on Paul's command to "present your bodies as a living sacrifice, holy and acceptable to God, which is your spiritual worship" (Romans 12:1). Because we belong to him, body and soul, we strive by the Spirit's power to live each day out of our new blood-bought reality. As Sam Allberry concludes:

> In any other context, hearing that we are not our
> own, that we have been bought with a price, would
> be devastating. It would indicate a lack of freedom,
> dignity, and worth. But when applied to Jesus, the
> opposite is the case. Belonging to him is the only way to
> true freedom. Nothing could be more dignifying. And
> nothing shows our worth more than Jesus shedding his
> own blood for us. To belong to him is the highest and
> greatest blessing we could ever hope for.[50]

CHAPTER ELEVEN

OTHERS
Relational Spaces

"It is a serious thing to live in a society of possible gods and goddesses, to remember that the dullest and most uninteresting person you can talk to may one day be a creature which, if you saw it now, you would be strongly tempted to worship, or else a horror and a corruption such as you now meet, if at all, only in a nightmare. All day long we are, in some degree, helping each other to one or other of these destinations. It is in the light of these overwhelming possibilities, it is with the awe and the circumspection proper to them, that we should conduct all our dealings with one another, all friendships, all loves, all play, all politics. There are no ordinary people. You have never talked to a mere mortal."

C.S. LEWIS

We all know a person or two in our lives who is just naturally more attentive to those around them. When out in public, they tend to not just see *people*—an amorphous group of strangers whose faces blur together in one large sea of humanity—but *persons*. Particular human beings, with a name and a story. Persons, who matter to God.

Our eldest son, Benaiah, is one of those humans with a natural, God-given capacity for seeing *people* as *persons*. I can remember one occasion when he was five or six years old.

We were driving through our city with our whole family in the car. There was a local election taking place, so naturally there were numerous people on sidewalks and out the front of public buildings, lining up to cast their votes. Benaiah had been talking but then suddenly grew quiet, staring out of the window while counting under his breath. After a minute or so of this, my wife, Kristina, asked if everything was okay. Benaiah took a moment and then turned to meet her eyes from the backseat of the car. "Mum," he said, with eyes wide and worry etched into his young face, "there are just so many lost people in our city. I can't even count them all!"

Kristina and I locked eyes. Our hearts melted. I briefly entertained the idea of writing a parenting book on how to raise child-evangelists.

"Look, there's one," he said. "And there's one. And there's another one!"

It then dawned on us: our son was pointing at election campaign posters. He had mistaken them for pictures of "missing persons"— "lost" like a dog or a cat that had run away—and thought that all these people were out on the streets desperately trying to find them.

We chuckled as we explained to him that those were pictures of politicians, even as I chuckle now at the memory. But the truth is I want to be more like my son in the way he sees those around them. I am still learning to see *people* as *persons*. Faithful presence means that we measure the wealth of our lives by the depths of our relationships. It means living with our eyes open to not only just the tasks we need to complete, but to the persons whom we live among.

THERE YOU ARE!
I've heard it said that there are two ways to walk into a room. One says, "Here I am!" while the other says, "There you are!" One looks like the Pharisees, parading their self-perceived

greatness. The other looks like Jesus, who said, *There you are!* to a sceptical Nathanael sitting under a tree (John 1:45-48), and to a woman at a well who was looking for love in all the wrong places (4:7-42), and to a loathed tax collector named Zacchaeus (Luke 19:5). For these people and countless more, Jesus saw them, moved toward them, spoke truth to them and welcomed them. That's what love looks like. How he has loved us is how he wants us to love others.

Jesus made clear that the next most important commandment after loving God with our whole selves (Mark 12:30) is loving our neighbours as much as ourselves (v 31). Even more costly than neighbour love, Jesus calls us to follow him into the difficult work of enemy love (Matthew 5:44). Between our neighbours and our enemies, that should just about cover *everyone we cross paths with.* How are we meant to do *that?* While God is omnipresent— fully attentive and present to not only every *where* of place but every *when* of time—when God the Son took on a body, he took on the limitations of life in that body. That included relational limitations. Like us, Jesus could only be present to one person or group of persons at a time.

Perhaps, like me, you want to be more relationally present to those around you. You don't want to jet-ski along the surface of your relationships; you want to dive deeper into the waters of belonging and the joy that comes with being truly known yet authentically cherished. Yet all of this raises some important questions when it comes to the limits of our horizontal relationships. *How many people can I be meaningfully attentive to? And who am I meant to relationally prioritise?*

MAKING PEACE WITH RELATIONAL LIMITATIONS
As we saw in the previous chapter, the intimacy of belonging requires us to embrace the limitations that come with

belonging. To belong to God means to make our home in worshipping him alone. To belong to a place requires limiting yourself to that place and giving your loving attention to it. And the same is true of our horizontal relationships with other people.

To belong to another person, in the context of love, is to willingly limit yourself by practising faithful presence with them (and, by necessity, being non-present to others).

Our relationships are not so much "places" as they are "spaces". Places limit our geographic presence, while spaces speak to our relational presence. And the truth is, depending on the season of life we're in and our own relational capacity, there are a limited number of relational spaces that we can meaningfully inhabit. It's not that we have a figure in mind—a clearly defined relational quota—that, once reached, turns the sign on the front of our lives from *Open* to *No Vacancy*. It's just that we are limited by the hours in each day and the number of places we can be. At a certain point, unique to each of us, every new relationship added into our lives will either be diminished in quality itself or will flourish into something beautiful and fruit-bearing but thus diminishing the quality of another relationship that is not as highly cultivated.

Maybe you're familiar with Dunbar's number, also known as the Rule of 150?

A British anthropologist and professor at Oxford named Robin Dunbar spent decades studying the complexities of friendships and discovered that the number of people we can maintain some sort of meaningful relationship with at any given point in our lives is somewhere between 100 and 250 people, with an average of 150. Historically, the Rule of 150 rule characterises the general size of most hunter-gatherer tribes, neolithic villages and medieval English villages. It is the typical community size of the Hutterites and of Native Americans, the average number in a company of fighting soldiers (like the U.S. Marines) and the attendance at an average wedding.[51]

In other words, Dunbar was on to something. We are relationally limited creatures.

There are only so many relational spaces we can faithfully inhabit. While we most certainly can practise faithful presence to others in a general way as we go about our lives, the New Testament reveals four specific relational spaces that we can cultivate intentionally: our household, our church, our friendships and our witness.

FAITHFUL PRESENCE IN OUR HOUSEHOLD

While the New Testament emphasises marriage as the most intimate of human relationships, and gives important instructions for husbands, wives, and children alike when it comes to their life together as a family (Ephesians 5:22 – 6:9; Colossians 3:18-21; Titus 2:1-5), the language most frequently used to refer to the space that these dynamics played out in is not the language of a *family* but of a *household*. To be sure, there is overlap between the two. But they are not the same. Today, many families don't live in the same household. And many households are made up of persons who are not related to one another by blood. In the New Testament, a household included not only the immediate members of a family but everyone who lived under that roof, which often included extended family and bondservants. Interestingly, in each of the above passages, Paul gives explicit instructions on how *every* member of a Christian household was to treat one another (see also Ephesians 6:5-9; Colossians 3:22 – 4:1; Titus 2:6-10).

In his outstanding book *The Life We're Looking For*, Andy Crouch defines the household as "the first and most important canopy of trust we need to thrive as human beings—a place where we can always go, a place where we are safe enough to sleep".[52] The members of a household have a shared life and set of responsibilities by virtue of their intimate sharing of place. Crouch describes the importance of this interconnectedness when he writes:

> A household is both place and people—or maybe better, it is a particular people with a particular place. A household is a community of persons who may well take shelter under one roof but also and more fundamentally take shelter under one another's care and concern. They provide for one another, and they depend on one another … The household is the fundamental community of persons.[53]

Whether we live in a house with just our immediate family or share accommodation with a handful of friends or room-mates, the relational space of our homes is the first place where we are to be faithfully present. Here, we experience the limits of a shared life together. Here, we both learn and practise the relational ebbs and flows of trust, repentance, forgiveness and sacrifice.

For those of us who are parents, it means taking every opportunity we have through our children's pre-adult lives to look them in their eyes and remind them that they are seen and accepted—a daily "There you are!" in which they are recognised and cherished. The old parenting adage is true: love to a child is spelt T-I-M-E. But it also might be spelt S-E-E-N. The same is true for all our relationships in the home; the household is the primary place where faithful presence is to be practised.

FAITHFUL PRESENCE IN OUR CHURCH

In light of the above, it is interesting that the church is sometimes called "the household of God" (Ephesians 2:19; 1 Timothy 3:15; 1 Peter 4:17). And God cares deeply about how those in a household give themselves to one another. Look at the way the Scriptures call us to prioritise the relational space of our local church: "So then, as we have opportunity, let us do good to everyone, and especially to those who are of the household of faith" (Galatians 6:10). We are to be attentive to the good we can do for everyone as we have opportunity, but *especially so* when it comes to one another in the church. Consider the following (by no means exhaustive) list of "one anothers" in the New Testament, and the impossibility of practising and experiencing each of these without authentic relational proximity:

Love one another (John 13:34).
Outdo one another in showing honour (Romans 12:10).
Rejoice with one another (Romans 12:15).
Live in harmony with one another (Romans 12:16).
Welcome one another (Romans 15:7).
Serve one another (Galatians 5:13).
Be patient with one another (Ephesians 4:2).
Forgive one another (Ephesians 4:32).
Submit to one another (Ephesians 5:21).
Bear with one another (Colossians 3:13).
Teach one another (Colossians 3:16).
Encourage one another (1 Thessalonians 4:18).
Build one another up (1 Thessalonians 5:11).
Pray for one another (James 5:16).

Perhaps one question that each of us who love Jesus would do well to occasionally ask ourselves is: if everyone at my church treated the church the way I presently am, would that church be flourishing? When we read in Acts 2:42 that the early church "devoted themselves to the apostles' teaching and the fellowship, to the breaking of bread and the prayers", we are reading of a people who viewed their togetherness with one another as *anything but* casual or optional.

In fact, according to Jesus, his followers' faithful presence to one another is the defining, visible evidence of their faithfulness to him: "By this all people will know that you are my disciples, if you have love for one another" (John 13:35). When our churches become known for this—for loving one another with the same intensity and sacrificity that Christ has loved us with—they become a living sermon of the good news we cherish and proclaim.

Our presence to one another is of unimaginable significance. On Sunday morning, you are never just showing up to a service. You are participating in a community that is not only shaping you and spurring you onward toward your eternal future but one that is previewing that future by your togetherness in the gospel as the people of God!

Paul reminds believers in Rome that they simultaneously imitate and exalt Jesus when they "welcome one another as Christ has welcomed [them], for the glory of God" (Romans 15:7). One of the best texts I've received as a pastor came from a church member whose heart had been awakened to this Romans 15:7 reality:

> We've come to realise that "our house" isn't ours at all, it's one of the many gifts God has given us that we are to use as tools in fulfilling the "one another" instructions of the New Testament. (When people come over, we tell them they have "fridge rights"). We've seen our house become a place where we can love, serve, confess our sins to one another … outdo one another in honour, etc. As the saying goes, "When you have more than you need, build a longer table, not a higher fence".

So go ahead and think about those men and women with whom you gather to exalt Jesus on a Sunday. What names and faces is the Spirit bringing to mind right now as you do? What gaps within your church's shared life together could your presence fill? In what ways is God calling you to prioritise or reprioritise your attention when it comes to your brothers and sisters in the household of God?

FAITHFUL PRESENCE IN OUR FRIENDSHIPS

One of the tricks that social media has played on us all is making us think that we have more meaningful relationships than we actually do. For example, right now, Facebook tells me that I have just under 5,000 friends. But I know the truth: the real number of friends in my life is probably closer to about 0.25% of that figure—somewhere around twelve people. In other words, 99.75% of the people that Facebook says are my friends, aren't.

And you know what? That's ok. The same basic principle is true for you as well.

Do you remember Dunbar's number? His research is actually better represented by a series of numbers that speak into the average human relational capacity. While 150 might be the number of meaningful relational connections we can have, the number of close and intimate friendships we can maintain is far, far fewer. Of those 150 people, Dunbar

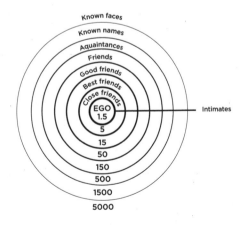

suggests that 50 of them would be the kind of friends we'd want at a weekend barbecue, and of that 50, only 15 would be the kind of friends we regularly hang out with and perhaps trust with our children. And of those 15, only five would be the kind of people we know would drop everything for us when our world falls apart.[54]

The deeper and more intimate the friendship, the fewer of those friends we will have.

I have shared the story of one of my friends named Alex in a previous book.[55] A few years ago, I had received some difficult news about a complicated, challenging leadership crisis that was about to go very public and through which I would have to lead others in the church. I shot Alex a text saying little more than that and asked for prayer. Within a minute, a voice message appeared on my phone: "Hey. Are you in trouble? I will get on the next airplane and be wherever I need to be. Whatever you need. All that's mine is yours, I've got your back, no matter what. I love you, Adam."

Perhaps not all of us will have a friend like Alex. But all of us, in light of how greatly we have been loved by Jesus, should desire to become a friend like that—a friend who is faithfully present, no matter what. Friendships like these don't just happen. They are formed by presence and sustained by attentiveness. Their diamond-like strength comes from being forged through pressure and trials that the friends have endured together. And when, over time, we find ourselves experiencing a friendship or two of this calibre, we enter into an experience of our heavenly future in the present that is unspeakably precious.

FAITHFUL PRESENCE IN OUR WITNESS

One final area of relational responsibility that is worth considering intentionally is our witness. After Jesus rose from the grave and before he ascended into glory, he left his followers with a holy responsibility that we commonly call the Great Commission:

> *Go therefore and make disciples of all nations.*
> *(Matthew 28:19)*

> *But you will receive power when the Holy Spirit has come upon you, and you will be my witnesses in Jerusalem and in all Judea and Samaria, and to the ends of the earth.*
> *(Acts 1:8)*

To be a witness is to simply pass on what you have heard, seen and experienced. As Christians, we have heard the gospel—the greatest news on earth: that God has done for us what we could not do for ourselves, adopting us into his family on the merits of the life, death and resurrection of Jesus. Living faithfully in the evangelistic spaces of our lives is costly, but it isn't complicated. Our part in God's mission can be simplified into two vital realities: the rhythms we live out and the household we live in.

First, where you are right now is where God intends to bring good news. He may send you across the world, but the world is not your personal responsibility. Your responsibility is the relational spheres you inhabit each and every normal day of your life. God has sovereignly embedded us in our present neighbourhoods and workplaces and schools and cities for the sake of his name. In this way, mission is not necessarily going somewhere new; it's being attentive to the opportunities that the Spirit leads us into where we are. Mission is not an extra programme we try to squeeze into our busy life but a lens through which we see all of life. Being faithfully present as a witness to Jesus Christ means that we prioritise walking out the normal rhythms of present life, in our present place, with gospel intentionality. Writing about the early church in the 1st century, the historian Kenneth S. Latourette remarks that "the primary change agents in the spread of faith … were the men and women who earned their livelihood in some purely secular manner, and spoke of their faith to those whom they met in this natural fashion".[56] They weren't experts but just courageously available.

Second, God's mission for many of us will include the places where we sit down to eat and drink. Paul reminds us to "be joyful in hope, patient in affliction, faithful in prayer. Share with the Lord's people who are in need. Practise hospitality. Bless those who persecute you; bless and do not curse" (Romans 12:12-14, NIV). The Greek word used here for "hospitality" is *philoxenia*, which breaks down into "love toward strangers". What Paul is describing is an openness of life to outsiders, which intentionally invites them in. Rosaria Butterfield—who herself was converted from a radically anti-Christian worldview to become a faithful follower of Christ—reminds us that "the hospitable meet people as strangers and invite them to become neighbours, and, by God's grace, many will go on to become part of the family of God".[57]

What might it look like for you to use your home as a space for gospel storytelling, hospitality and neighbour love? It might look like spending more time in the front yard than the backyard or putting out an extra plate of food or two along with a thoughtful invitation to those around you to come and share a meal. It might mean entering your favourite coffee shop with more attentiveness—more eye contact and less AirPods. It might mean building more margin into your busy schedule so that you can be interrupted by the providential opportunities that God sends your way. God's mission, and our participation in it, is not "out there" somewhere. It's right here, among the names and faces and places in our present.

CHAPTER TWELVE

ETERNITY
Heavenly Places

"Nothing is more often misdiagnosed than our homesickness for Heaven. We think that what we want is sex, drugs, alcohol, a new job, a raise, a doctorate, a spouse, a large-screen television, a new car, a cabin in the woods, a condo in Hawaii. What we really want is the person we were made for, Jesus, and the place we were made for, Heaven. Nothing less can satisfy us."

RANDY ALCORN

It's hard for us to wrap our minds around eternity. Or any great length of time, for that matter. For example, when we hear words like *thousand, million, billion* and *trillion,* we might have a tendency to think of them as evenly spaced markers along a numerical ruler. But when we examine these words in the context of time, it quickly becomes apparent how poorly we grasp their vastness.

A thousand seconds means that a little over 16.5 minutes has passed.

A million seconds is the equivalent of 11.5 days.

So far, none of that is too shocking. But what if I told you that to experience a billion seconds is to experience everything that took place from the day you were born to a little after your 31st birthday? Thirty-one years.

And a trillion seconds? That would be thirty-one thousand,

six hundred and eighty-eight years. Not days. Not months. *Years*. 31,688 of them. And that just gets you to one trillion *seconds*. If we were to try and measure one trillion in days or months, the numerical quantity would become unfathomable.

Yet even a trillion *centuries* will be little more than the opening of the door into an infinite beyond when considered in the larger context of eternity.

As we've explored the God-given limitations of our time and place through this book, I've tried to show how being convinced of our definite future in Christ empowers faithfulness in the here and now. Yet, for some of us, the thought of a never-ending future feels a little, well, daunting. Like preparing to step out of a plane with a parachute for the first time, when we stare at the unknown and unexplored reality of infinite time, our brain struggles to comprehend the sheer vastness of eternity's horizon—let alone look forward to it.

But what if, when we thought of eternity, we saw it more through the lens of kairos than chronos? Not merely as unending seconds but as such perfect and perpetual fullness that we won't even consider those seconds? Not only as *everlasting* life but everlasting *life*.

Like unhurried laughter with friends or being lost in thoughts of wonder, when the kairos of such beautiful times eclipses every thought of clock time. Like when we have a rare perfect moment when beauty and meaning and presence and love all seem to collide, and we are captivated by the sheer *rightness* of it all, wishing somehow with every fibre of our being that *this* moment could be stretched out for ever. Even the best moments in this life are corrupted with the knowledge of their inevitable ending. Eternal life, however, as C.S. Lewis describes it at the end of his Chronicles of Narnia, is that in which "every chapter is better than the one before".[58] It is perfect and meaningful fullness—which somehow only gets fuller and more meaningful the further we plunge into it. Goodness of that potency is beyond our comprehension. Can such a place really exist?

The Bible speaks of such a time and place: *heaven*. And deep down, every one of us longs for it with a cosmic homesickness, for God "has put eternity into [our] heart" (Ecclesiastes 3:11). When we think of the concepts of place and space, rarely does the place known as "heaven" come to mind. But if we are to be a faithful presence in this world, then heaven is exactly what we need to have more on our minds.

BEING HEAVENLY MINDED *FOR* EARTHLY GOOD

Perhaps you've heard the silly saying, "Don't be so heavenly minded that you're of no earthly good". The truth is that for most of us, our real problem is the opposite: an earthly-mindedness that blinds us to our eternal future and paralyses us with anxiety in the present because our tendency is to treat this life as ultimate. Seriously, when was the last time you spent even 20 continuous minutes thinking about heaven? C.S. Lewis reminds us that it is, in fact, a robust heavenly-mindedness that empowers great earthly good:

> A continual looking forward to the eternal world is not (as some modern people think) a form of escapism or wishful thinking, but one of the things a Christian is meant to do. It does not mean that we are to leave the present world as it is. If you read history you will find that the Christians who did most for the present world were just those who thought most of the next. The Apostles themselves, who set on foot the conversion of the Roman Empire, the great men who built up the Middle Ages, the English Evangelicals who abolished the Slave Trade, all left their mark on Earth, precisely because their minds were occupied with Heaven. It is

since Christians have largely ceased to think of the other world that they have become so ineffective in this.[59]

Heaven and earth were made together and made for each other—they're not in opposition to one another. "In the beginning, God created the *heavens* and the earth" (Genesis 1:1; see also Nehemiah 9:6). The former is the plumb line for the latter, which is why Jesus taught his disciples to pray to the Father, "Your kingdom come, your will be done, on earth as it is in heaven" (Matthew 6:10). Heaven and earth, according to the theologian Tom Wright, "are the twin interlocking spheres of God's single created reality. You only really understand earth when you are equally familiar with heaven."[60] To create a dichotomy that diminishes our attentiveness to either earth or heaven is to separate what the Scriptures join together. If we are to truly pray with Jesus that God's "will be done, on earth as it is in heaven", then we need to have some understanding of the heavenly places that we are called to replicate on earth.

Which raises the question, "What is heaven anyway?"

THE PRESENT HEAVEN: LIFE AFTER DEATH

When many of us hear the word "heaven", we tend to immediately think of the place that Christians go to when they die, this side of Christ's return. Some will assume that "life after death" is an eternal disembodied reality, where our souls are gathered to God, and that we'll spend eternity as spiritual beings in our spiritual location, called "heaven". The first sentence of this paragraph is true; the second is false.

Heaven *is* where Christians this side of Christ's return go when they die. But heaven *is not*, in its present form, eternal. Don't get me wrong: it's better than anything we have ever experienced or could ever imagine. We will be free from the destructive presence of sin, and we will be with God, in whose "presence there is fullness of joy" (Psalm 16:11). But in its magnificent, current form, heaven is temporary. Randy Alcorn uses the terms "the present heaven" and "the eternal heaven"[61] to distinguish between the place where God presently dwells with the angels, along with believers who have died, and the new creation that will be inaugurated at the end of this present age when Christ returns.

So, before we move on to think about what heaven will be like eternally, let's briefly explore what heaven is like right now and why that matters for the way we live in this world. There's a lot we can speculate about, but here are three biblical realities that we can be certain about.

First, heaven is unspeakably wonderful. I mean that literally. When Paul was caught up to the present heaven, "he heard things that cannot be told, which man may not utter ... So to keep me from becoming conceited because of the surpassing greatness of the revelations, a thorn was given me in the flesh, a messenger of Satan to harass me" (2 Corinthians 12:4, 7). In other words, Paul's experience of the present heaven was so far beyond what we could imagine that he was forbidden to speak of it and given a thorn in the flesh to keep him from becoming conceited about it (which is one reason why any new "I went to heaven" book that dubiously seeks to add to our biblical knowledge of heaven causes me to nearly injure myself with excessive eye-rolling). Truly, "no eye has seen, nor ear heard, nor the heart of man imagined, what God has prepared for those who love him" (1 Corinthians 2:9). But whatever it's like, we can be certain that none of us will be disappointed.

Second, heaven is the present dwelling of every person, from the beginning of time until now, who trusted God by placing their faith in him. When we who belong to Jesus die, our mortal bodies go into the ground, while our spirits, reconciled to God, go directly and immediately to the present heaven. As Paul writes, to "be away from the body [is to be] at home with the Lord" (2 Corinthians 5:8). His desire was "to depart and *be with Christ*, for that is far better" (Philippians 1:23, emphasis added). Those in the present heaven with Christ are at rest, experiencing fullness of joy, even as they seem to be aware of what is happening on earth, both as a "great cloud of witnesses" to the race set before us (Hebrews 12:1-2) and as those who experience "joy in heaven" when a sinner repents (Luke 15:7, 10). They are beholding in awe God's plan of redemption unfolding.

Third, and most important of all, heaven is the place of God's throne. The Lord says through Isaiah, "Heaven is my throne, and the earth is my footstool" (Isaiah 66:1). John saw Jesus seated on a throne in heaven, being honoured and worshipped by every angel, creature and person (Revelation 4). A throne is where the king sits, and from the throne, the king rules his kingdom. Jesus used the phrases "kingdom of God" and "kingdom of heaven" interchangeably because they are one and the same. The kingdom of heaven is under the perfect rule of God, which is why Jesus taught us to pray, "Your kingdom come, your will be done, on earth as it is in heaven" (Matthew 6:10).

Right now, we live as citizens of *that* kingdom: a faithful presence of the heavenly kingdom, who show this world what life looks like under the sovereign care and rule of our great King. We live in the "already/not yet"—God's kingdom is *already* breaking into this world through the lives of his people, but Christ has *not yet* returned to bring God's kingdom, fully and finally, "on earth as it is in heaven". And when that day comes, we will *really* enter into the fullness of God's eternal promise—into the eternal heaven rather than the present heaven. Or, as Wright insightfully describes it, into "life *after* life after death".[62]

THE NEW CREATION: LIFE *AFTER* LIFE AFTER DEATH

So what will "life after life after death" be like? Answering this question about our future is essential to faithfulness in our present. And in Christ, the future of both our bodies and our world is renewal. Read the following passages slowly so that your imagination about that future has a biblical shape.

> *⁶ On this mountain the LORD of hosts will make for all peoples*
> *a feast of rich food, a feast of well-aged wine,*
> *of rich food full of marrow, of aged wine well refined.*
>
> *⁷ And he will swallow up on this mountain*
> *the covering that is cast over all peoples,*
> *the veil that is spread over all nations.*
>
> *⁸ He will swallow up death for ever;*
> *and the Lord GOD will wipe away tears from all faces,*
> *and the reproach of his people he will take away from all the earth,*
> *for the LORD has spoken.*
>
> *⁹ It will be said on that day,*
> *"Behold, this is our God; we have waited for him, that he might save us.*
> *This is the LORD; we have waited for him;*
> *let us be glad and rejoice in his salvation." (Isaiah 25:6-9)*

Notice that it is not God's people that are taken away from the earth but their "reproach" (v 8)—our sin and its cursed consequences. Also notice the embodied earthiness of that perfected eternal life: Isaiah's words are bursting with joy and song and feasting, as the Lord himself throws a victory banquet when death is finally and irreversibly put to death. The apostle John describes a similar scene:

> *Then I saw a new heaven and a new earth, for the first*

*heaven and the first earth had passed away, and the sea was
no more. And I saw the holy city, new Jerusalem, coming
down out of heaven from God, prepared as a bride adorned
for her husband. And I heard a loud voice from the throne
saying, "Behold, the dwelling place of God is with man.
He will dwell with them, and they will be his people, and
God himself will be with them as their God. He will wipe
away every tear from their eyes, and death shall be no more,
neither shall there be mourning, nor crying, nor pain any
more, for the former things have passed away." And he who
was seated on the throne said, "Behold, I am making all
things new." Also he said, "Write this down, for these words
are trustworthy and true." (Revelation 21:1-5)*

To be sure, there is newness of life as the old passes away—a
new heaven and a new earth as God himself makes all things
new—but there is also continuity with what was. John Piper
points out that this "passing away" does not necessarily mean
heaven and earth will go out of existence "but may mean
that there will be such a change in them that their present
condition passes away. We might say, 'The caterpillar passes
away, and the butterfly emerges.' There is a real passing away,
and there is a real continuity, a real connection."[63]

It may help to think of the newness in the language of
salvation. Paul says, "If anyone is in Christ, he is a new
creation. The old has passed away; behold, the new has
come" (2 Corinthians 5:17). Becoming a Christian doesn't
mean you ceased to be *you*. You are still you yet gloriously
new. And so it will be with this world. It will still be this
world but gloriously new. Renewed. Which is why Paul,
in Romans 8:19-23, describes creation as groaning in
anticipation, waiting in hope, longing to "be set free from
the bondage to decay into the glorious freedom of God's
children" (v 21, CSB).

Think of the most beautiful place on earth you've ever seen. Can you picture it? Or perhaps a photo of some place at the top of your travel bucket list. Consider the majesty of the Swiss Alps or the Grand Canyon; the white sands and shallow waters of Fiji or the Maldives, which sparkle with unbelievable blueness; the rolling green hills of the Welsh countryside; the sunflower fields of Tuscany; the jungles of the Congo and the rainforests of the Amazon; the enchanted fjords of Norway or the sunsets of Hawaii.

What you've envisaged is merely the cursed version of those places.

There is coming a day when heaven will come down and clothe this present world with resurrection glory, and the people of God "shall go out in joy and be led forth in peace; the mountains and the hills before you shall break forth into singing, and all the trees of the field shall clap their hands" (Isaiah 55:12). On that day, creation itself will join the party and celebrate with us, as it is finally restored to be what it once was: a dwelling place for humanity that radiates with the glory of God.

So, rather than saying, "This world is not my home," we should say instead, "This world, *as it is right now*, is not my home. But it will be." The first has the capacity to lead us to an escapist mentality that just wants to get out of this broken world; the second leads to a mindset by which we attentively live in this world as ambassadors of Christ and agents of restoration, for we know that the God who made us new is right now "making all things new" (Revelation 21:5). For the hope at the heart of the gospel is not merely that we will escape God's righteous wrath (though we certainly will!) but that we are made new. And so it will be with the world as we know it. Every delight, sight, sense, satisfaction and beauty will be amplified beyond our wildest dreams. Every evil, suffering, injustice and tear will be forever wiped away. On that unspeakably precious day, never again will our hearts grieve the injustice of cancer or the cancer of injustice. Never again will our hearts break from loneliness or betrayal. We will inhabit a renewed world where there are no more children's hospitals or emergency rooms; no more chronic pain or crippling anxiety; no more SWAT teams or security guards; no more terrorist attacks or panic attacks; no more funerals or fear or violence or sin, for "death shall be no more" (Revelation 21:4)!

That, dear friend, is where we are heading in Christ. Eternity will be a new time, in a renewed place, in which every promise that God has made will be perfectly fulfilled (and then some). Right now, then, "according to his promise we are waiting for new heavens and a new earth in which righteousness dwells" (2 Peter 3:13). We are to live in our present time and place as citizens of *that* future.

INHABITING THE PRESENT AS CITIZENS OF THE FUTURE
The New Testament portrays those who are destined to share in Christ's resurrection as "strangers and exiles" (1 Peter 2:11, CSB), "foreigners and temporary residents on the earth" (Hebrews 11:13, CSB), who are "looking for a better place, a heavenly homeland" (v 16, NLT). Each of those phrases describes displaced people: women and men who belong to *another* place, even as they temporarily inhabit their present one.

But despite the unsettledness and tension that marks so much of our present experience, we are to remember that our ultimate allegiance is to the kingdom of God and our future heavenly homeland. We are citizens of *that* kingdom— citizens of the future world. While the world will certainly see faithful believers as out of step with the times, Paul reminds us that "our citizenship is in heaven" (Philippians 3:20), and urges believers, "as citizens of heaven, [to] live your life worthy of the gospel of Christ" (1:27, CSB). What does a life like that look like?

About 20 to 30 years after the apostle John had passed away—the last living witness to the life, death and resurrection of Jesus—a letter from an unnamed author was written to a Roman named Diognetus explaining Christianity and the rapid spread of the gospel across the known world. This important letter reveals how 2nd-century believers practised faithful presence in the midst of a hostile world:

> [Christians] dwell in their own countries, but simply as sojourners. As citizens, they share in all things with others and yet endure all things as if foreigners. Every foreign land is to them as their native country, and every land of their birth as a land of strangers. They marry, as do all [others]; they beget children; but they do not destroy their offspring. They have a common table, but not a common bed. They are in the flesh, but they do not live after the flesh. They pass their days on earth but they are citizens of heaven. They obey the prescribed laws, and at the same time surpass the laws by their lives. They love all men, and are persecuted by all.[64]

What might our lives look like if, as these early Christians did, we were to truly order our lives according to our blood-bought heavenly identity? John Piper reminds us that when we know and believe the truth about the future, "that truth makes you free indeed. Free from the short, shallow, suicidal pleasures of sin, and free for the sacrifices of mission and ministry that cause people to give glory to our Father in heaven."[65] Our citizenship in heaven makes the worst times in this world liveable and the best times in this world leaveable, because our hope is not ultimately tied to anything in this present world. We are citizens of the world to come, inhabiting the world that is as participants in God's plan of redemption and as living evidence that he is indeed accomplishing that plan. In fact, mission is the process through which realities that are true of heaven are becoming evident on earth through the people of God: in our proclamation of the gospel and the Spirit-empowered distinctiveness of our lives.

It is no surprise, then, that at the end of 1 Corinthians 15— Paul's chapter on the resurrection of Christ and the resurrection in our own future—he closes the chapter by concluding, "Therefore, my beloved brothers, be steadfast, immovable, always abounding in the work of the Lord, knowing that in the Lord your labour is not in vain" (v 58). In other words: *Christians, our work in the present has eternal ramifications. Nothing you do for the Lord is ever wasted. Don't lose heart; everything matters.*

EPILOGUE
Time Unlimited in Place Uncursed

"Now suppose both death and hell were utterly defeated.
Suppose the fight was fixed. Suppose God took you on a crystal
ball trip into your future and you saw with indubitable
certainty that despite everything—your sin, your smallness,
your stupidity—you could have free for the asking your whole
crazy heart's deepest desire: heaven, eternal joy. Would you not
return fearless and singing? What can earth do to you, if you are
guaranteed heaven? To fear the worst earthly loss would be like
a millionaire fearing the loss of a penny—less,
a scratch on a penny."

PETER KREEFT

This side of glory, even the sweetest moments are laced
with the sorrow that they are not permanent.

I write these words from one of my favourite places in
the world, the Isle of Skye. To say it's beautiful doesn't quite
do it justice; it is majestic and rugged and mysterious and
enchanted. There are hues of green laced with bronze and
golds, and flowers wild and purple—colours and quietude
that feel as though they belong more to a fantasy landscape
like that of C.S. Lewis's *Perelandra* than they do to this world.

But this place *is* part of this world. And merely the cursed
version, at that. One day, Skye—along with the rest of this

created world—will groan no more for liberation from sin's curse, which has affected all of creation. One day, the world as we know it, including our bodies, will experience Christ's final promise of glorious renewal (Romans 8:18-21).

As I stand here gazing at the autumn glory of Skye, on the brink of stepping into the autumn years of my own life, I am struck by the promise of renewal in Jesus' words:

Behold, I am making all things new. (Revelation 21:5)

Here, the risen Jesus speaks in the present tense because he speaks to us from outside of time. To him, all of time is the present. He alone can claim the title of "I AM", for he alone always *is*. The present is where he always will be, and it exists only because he is there. The present is God's eternal home. "'I am the Alpha and the Omega,' says the Lord God, 'who is and who was and who is to come, the Almighty'" (Revelation 1:8). And home with God is where each and every one of us who love Jesus is heading.

HEADING HOME

Today, I make the long journey home from Skye after a few days of hunting for words to fill these pages and wonder to fill my heart.

Home, where those I love most in God's world are.

Home, where God inhabits and glorifies the beautiful normality that makes up most of life.

Home, where God calls me to be faithfully present.

Still, saying goodbye to beauty is hard. But one day, we will say goodbye to all goodbyes. One day, death itself will die. One day, God will turn up the dial on the peak moments of bliss; the satisfaction that we experienced within time will become the new baseline for "normal life".

He will so intimately include you in himself and clothe you with his own glory that if present you were to meet future you, you would have to bow your head and shield your eyes. In fact, there are waves of joy in your future so far beyond your comprehension that God needs to strengthen your physical frame with a glorified body just for you to even have the capacity to handle the intensity of such happiness.

*In your presence there is **fullness** of joy; at your right hand are pleasures **for evermore**. (Psalm 16:11, my emphasis)*

That's where we're heading. And the God-given parameters of your body and time and place are what God has ordained to prepare you for that day without end. Your present limitations are part of your divinely ordained means of sanctification. You are being instructed in the school of faithfulness. So do not lament the shortness of your days or the changing of the seasons. Do not despair that you cannot freeze the best moments in time. Instead, press on in the power of the Holy Spirit, fully and gratefully alive to the short life God has given you. Receive each day as the limited-edition gift that it is. God does not promise you tomorrow. But he does promise you, in Christ, an everlasting life in his never-failing love.

And to truly love and be loved means embracing the limits that authentic love requires of us: that we are not our own but belong to another. We are *not* God and never can be God—and that's good news for every one of us, whenever we're ready to receive it. For when we make peace with our creatureliness—the brevity of our lives amid the brokenness of this world—looking to Jesus again and again and again as the Redeemer that all of creation is longing for, we discover that faithful presence is at the very heart of God's glorious cosmic plan. For after all, "faithfully present" is what God is to us. As author James Davison Hunter reminds us, God's faithful presence to us...

... is a quality of commitment that is active, not passive; intentional, not accidental; covenantal, not contractual. In the life of Christ we see how it entailed his complete attention. It is wholehearted, not half-hearted; focused and purposeful, nothing desultory about it. His very name, Immanuel, signifies all of this—"God with us"—in our presence (Matthew 1:23).[66]

And it's God's unchanging, faithful presence that will sustain you when your here and now feels blown about like a feather in a hurricane. The constant change of time and pressures of place need not haunt you when you know that your future is held secure by "the Father of lights with whom there is no variation or shadow due to change" (James 1:17). By faith alone, in an undeserved grace alone that is found in Christ alone, your life has been permanently entwined in his. In this present time, you will indeed be "grieved by various trials" (1 Peter 1:6). But God's promise to you in Christ is invincible: "After you have suffered for a little while, the God of all grace, who has called you to his eternal glory in Christ, will himself restore, confirm, strengthen, and establish you" (5:10).

Before long, probably sooner than you think, time as we presently understand it will be unlimited. Place as we now see it will be uncursed. We will inhabit resurrection bodies, in a resurrected world, with the one who said, "I am the resurrection and the life" (John 11:25). Being convinced of *that* future will empower you to be faithful in your present, here and now, wherever and whenever, to the glory of God.

Endnotes

1 World Cities Database, https://simplemaps.com/data/world-cities, (accessed September 17, 2022).

2 Zack Eswine, *The Imperfect Pastor* (Crossway, 2015), p 40.

3 Wendell Berry, *A Timbered Choir* (Random House US, 1999), p 178. Berry's thoughts and words feature frequently through the pages of this book; few over this past busy, anxious, and distracted century have argued with greater eloquence to being faithfully present to the time and place God has us in, than he.

4 James Davison Hunter, *To Change the World* (Oxford University Press, 2010), p 243-244.

5 Alex Early, https://www.redemptionseattle.com, (accessed September 17, 2022)

6 Irenaeus of Lyons, *Irenaeus against Heresies, in Ante-Nicene Christian Library, vol. 1, The Apostolic Fathers with Justin Martyr and Irenaeus,* trans. Alexander Roberts and James Donaldson (Christian Literature Company, 1885), p 490.

7 Vasily Grossman, *Life and Fate* (Vintage Books, 2006), p 35.

8 Morgan Housel, *The Psychology of Money* (Harriman House, 2020), p 12.

9 Anne Lamott, *All New People* (Counterpoint, 1989), p 117.

10 Seneca, *Letters from a Stoic* (Penguin Books, 1969), p 33.

11 Lewis Mumford, *Technics and Civilization* (The University of Chicago Press, 2010), p 13.

12 Neil Postman, *Amusing Ourselves to Death* (Penguin Books, 1985), p 11.

13 Ibid.

14 N.D Wilson, *Death by Living* (Thomas Nelson, 2013), p 107.

15 Laura Haas, *Soon and Very Soon (or, Teaching a Two-Year Old About Time)*, https://carrara.liberti.church/soon-and-very-soon/ (accessed February 15, 2023).

16 Ibid.

17 Anna Akhmatova, *Selected Poems* (Penguin Books, 2006), p 85.

18 John Mark Comer, *The Ruthless Elimination of Hurry* (Waterbrook, 2019), p 93.

19 Sam Allberry, *7 Myths about Singleness* (Crossway: 2019), p 139.

20 Martin Luther, *The Complete Sermons of Martin Luther, Volume 3* (Baker Books , 2000), p 115.

21 Tony Reinke, "3 Reasons We're Addicted to Digital Distraction", https://www.crossway.org/articles/3-reasons-were-addicted-to-digital-distraction/ (accessed November 20, 2022).

22 Tish Harrison Warren, *Liturgy of the Ordinary* (Intervarsity Press, 2016), p 152.

23 Eugene H. Peterson, *Working the Angles* (Eerdmans, 1987), p 82.

24 Abraham Joshua Heschel, *The Sabbath* (Farrar, Straus, and Giroux, 1951), p 38.

25 Heschel, p.13.

26 Pete Scazzero, *The Emotionally Healthy Leader* (Zondervan, 2015), p 144.

27 Mike Cosper, *Recapturing the Wonder* (Intervarsity Press, 2018), p 88.

28 St Augustine, *Confessions* (The Folio Society, 1993), p 175.

29 St Augustine, p 222.

30 St Augustine, p 176.

31 C.S Lewis, *Letters to Malcolm* (Collins, 1981), p 28-29.

32 Ray Ortlund, *Isaiah: God Saves Sinners* (Crossway, 2005), p 289-290.

33 J. C. Ryle, *Expository Thoughts on John, vol. 2* (Robert Carter & Brothers, 1878), p 269.

34 Timothy Keller, *On Death* (Hodder & Stoughton, 2020), p 1, 2-3.

35 Benjamin Breckinridge Warfield, *The Person and Work of Christ* (The Presbyterian and Reformed Publishing Company, 1970), p 116-117.

36 Scott Hubbard, "Lady Jane Grey," https://www.desiringgod.org/articles/the-teenage-martyr (accessed December 11, 2022).

37 Thomas Watson in I.D.E Thomas, *A Puritan Golden Treasury* (The Banner of Truth Trust, 1977), p 70.

38 Edward S. Casey, *The Fate of Place* (University of California Press, 1997), *ix*.

39 Zack Eswine, *The Imperfect Pastor* (Crossway, 2015), p 39.

40 Craig Bartholomew, *Where Mortals Dwell* (Baker Publishing, 2011), p 29.

41 Anthony Giddens, *The Consequences of Modernity* (Stanford University Press, 1990), p 18.

42 Bo Burnham, *Inside* (Netflix Special).

43 Chris Martin, *Terms of Service* (B&H Publishing, 2022), p 203.

44 Wendell Berry, "The Body and the Earth," in The Art of the Commonplace: The Agrarian Essays of Wendell Berry (Counterpoint, 2002), 117.

45 Eswine, p 73.

46 John W. Kleinig, *Wonderfully Made* (Lexham Press, 2021), p 32.

47 Augustine of Hippo, *Sermons on the Liturgical Seasons*, ed. Hermigild Dressler, trans. Mary Sarah Muldowney, vol.

38, *The Fathers of the Church* (The Catholic University of America Press, 1959), p 18-19.

48 Sam Allberry, *What God Has to Say about Our Bodies* (Crossway, 2021), p 18-19.

49 Alan Noble, *You Are Not Your Own* (Intervarsity Press, 2021), p 118.

50 Allberry, p 136.

51 Robin Dunbar, *Friends: Understanding the Power of our Most Important Relationships* (Little, Brown Book Group, 2021), p 36 (Kindle Edition).

52 Andy Crouch, *The Life We're Looking For* (Convergent Books, 2022), p 140.

53 Crouch, 127-128.

54 Robin Dunbar, "You Can Only Maintain So Many Close Friendships," https://www.theatlantic.com/family/archive/2021/05/robin-dunbar-explains-circles-friendship-dunbars-number/618931/ (accessed December 21, 2022).

55 Adam Ramsey, *Truly, Truly, I Say to You* (The Good Book Company, 2023), p 119.

56 Kenneth S. Latourette, *A History of the Expansion of Christianity, Vol. 1* (Harper and Brothers, 1945), p 116.

57 Rosaria Butterfield, *The Gospel Comes with a House Key* (Crossway, 2018), p 50.

58 C.S. Lewis, *The Last Battle* (Lions, 1956), p 172.

59 C.S Lewis, *Mere Christianity* (Macmillan, 1952), p 118.

60 Tom Wright, *Surprised by Hope* (SPCK Publishing, 2007), p 263.

61 Randy Alcorn, *Heaven* (Tyndale, 2007), p 44.

62 Wright, *Surprised by Hope*, p 163.

63 John Piper, *Future Grace* (Multnomah Books, 1995), p 376.

64 "The Epistle to Diognetus", trans. Joseph Barber Lightfoot and J. R. Harmer, *The Apostolic Fathers* (Macmillan and

Co., 1891), p 506.

65 Piper, *Future Grace*, p 370.

66 James Davison Hunter, *To Change the World* (Oxford University Press, 2010), p 243.

BIBLICAL | RELEVANT | ACCESSIBLE

At The Good Book Company, we are dedicated to helping Christians and local churches grow. We believe that God's growth process always starts with hearing clearly what he has said to us through his timeless word—the Bible.

Ever since we opened our doors in 1991, we have been striving to produce Bible-based resources that bring glory to God. We have grown to become an international provider of user-friendly resources to the Christian community, with believers of all backgrounds and denominations using our books, Bible studies, devotionals, evangelistic resources, and DVD-based courses.

We want to equip ordinary Christians to live for Christ day by day, and churches to grow in their knowledge of God, their love for one another, and the effectiveness of their outreach.

Call us for a discussion of your needs or visit one of our local websites for more information on the resources and services we provide.

Your friends at The Good Book Company

thegoodbook.com | thegoodbook.co.uk
thegoodbook.com.au | thegoodbook.co.nz
thegoodbook.co.in